teach® yourself

writing a play

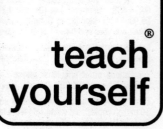

writing a play
lesley bown and
ann gawthorpe

For over 60 years, more than
50 million people have learnt over
750 subjects the **teach yourself**
way, with impressive results.

be where you want to be
with **teach yourself**

For UK order enquiries: please contact Bookpoint Ltd, 130 Milton Park, Abingdon, Oxon, OX14 4SB. Telephone: +44 (0) 1235 827720. Fax: +44 (0) 1235 400454. Lines are open 09.00–17.00, Monday to Saturday, with a 24-hour message answering service. Details about our titles and how to order are available at www.teachyourself.co.uk

For USA order enquiries: please contact McGraw-Hill Customer Services, PO Box 545, Blacklick, OH 43004-0545, USA. Telephone: 1-800-722-4726. Fax: 1-614-755-5645.

For Canada order enquiries: please contact McGraw-Hill Ryerson Ltd, 300 Water St, Whitby, Ontario, L1N 9B6, Canada. Telephone: 905 430 5000. Fax: 905 430 5020.

Long renowned as the authoritative source for self-guided learning – with more than 50 million copies sold worldwide – the **teach yourself** series includes over 500 titles in the fields of languages, crafts, hobbies, business, computing and education.

British Library Cataloguing in Publication Data: a catalogue record for this title is available from the British Library.

Library of Congress Catalog Card Number: on file.

First published in UK 2007 by Hodder Education, 338 Euston Road, London, NW1 3BH.

First published in US 2007 by The McGraw-Hill Companies, Inc.

This edition published 2007.

The **teach yourself** name is a registered trade mark of Hodder Headline.

Typeset by Transet Limited, Coventry, England.
Printed in Great Britain for Hodder Education, a division of Hodder Headline, an Hachette Livre UK Company, 338 Euston Road, London, NW1 3BH, by Cox & Wyman Ltd, Reading, Berkshire.

The publisher has used its best endeavours to ensure that the URLs for external websites referred to in this book are correct and active at the time of going to press. However, the publisher and the author have no responsibility for the websites and can make no guarantee that a site will remain live or that the content will remain relevant, decent or appropriate.

Hodder Headline's policy is to use papers that are natural, renewable and recyclable products and made from wood grown in sustainable forests. The logging and manufacturing processes are expected to conform to the environmental regulations of the country of origin.

Impression number   10 9 8 7 6 5 4 3 2 1
Year   2010 2009 2008 2007

contents

acknowledgments

x

Thank you to everybody who helped us with this book, and special thanks to John Bruce, John Colbourne, Ray Cooney, Abigail Davies, Jessica Dromgoule and Nicky Hudswell.

Lesley and Ann dedicate this book to their parents.

Can anyone write a play? Yes.

Can anyone be a successful writer? That will depend partly on talent, partly on luck but mostly on hard work. We all know that genius is 99 per cent perspiration and 1 per cent inspiration. Even inspiration can be helped along, and if you follow the practical advice given in this book, you will be able to write a play that works, and one that avoids the pitfalls that await most beginners.

There are many reasons why you may want to write a play. It could be you have always had a secret desire to be a writer, or perhaps you think you can do better than the last play you saw. Maybe you've been asked to do it, or maybe you've already tried and given up. Whatever your reasons for picking up this book, do persevere with your writing because there is nothing like the excitement of seeing your play performed for the first time.

The old joke says that there are three rules to writing a good play, but unfortunately no one knows what they are. This isn't quite true. There are clear rules about some aspects of playwriting, but there is always an example to be found of a writer who broke the rules and got away with it. Breaking the rules through ignorance rarely works, but deliberately flouting convention can be very successful. In other words, you can't break the rules till you know what they are.

Why we write

There are three basic reasons why people write:

- to enlighten
- to shock
- to entertain.

You may want to get across a particular message, such as that global warming has to be taken seriously. By incorporating that message into a play, it is possible to reach and inform people who might otherwise not be interested. If you think that, for example, society is breaking down, writing a play full of shocking images can have a tremendous impact. On the other hand, you may just wish to be entertaining and send the audience out with a happy glow.

There are three things to consider when writing a play – the three Ps.

- **Passion.** This can be a passion for theatre, a passion for writing, or a passion for one particular story. The best plays are written by people with all three types of passion.
- **Performance.** Plays are written to be performed, otherwise they have not fulfilled their function, and the writer won't have had the excitement of seeing their work produced.
- **Pragmatism.** Some people become writers almost by accident. If a script is needed, maybe for a school nativity play or a local pageant, and there is nobody to do it, a reluctant writer may come forward. If in the course of writing the script, they discover their passion, then they will go on to write more.

Using this book

The main aim of this book is to take you through the process of writing a stage play from beginning to end.

It also includes:

- practical information
- brief overviews of other types of drama
- information about placing a play
- a series of integrated exercises which will help you write a short dramatic scene
- contact details and useful websites in the Taking It Further section

- a script in development – so that you can watch a dramatic scene developing step-by-step we have developed our own Work In Progress, which is shown at the end of Chapters 01–09, with a full script at the end of the book.

Section 1 takes the reader through the whole process of writing a play – from where to get ideas to polishing and re-writes. There are chapters on characters, dialogue, plot construction and play analysis.

Section 2 explores the various play types and genres, with specific chapters on comedy, pantomime, musicals and writing for radio and television.

Section 3 explains the practical aspects of writing a script which is stageable and saleable, gives advice on placing a play and advice on putting on your own play.

Throughout the book, in line with one of the first rules of writing – 'show don't tell' – we have given brief examples from well-known plays and more detailed examples from our own plays. This is not to suggest that we have an overblown opinion of our own work, it's more that we understand it so well. Because we write simple comedies we've been able to find very straightforward examples, but these are still applicable to the most complex and subtle of dramas. We also, occasionally, give examples from well-known television programmes. Although television does not provide a good model for the stage writer, some aspects of storytelling and drama hold true whatever the medium, and television examples are readily accessible for those readers who haven't yet embarked on their theatre-going programme.

And finally...

No one can write for the stage unless they go and watch live theatre. Go to the theatre as much as possible and immerse yourself in the world of the stage. Try to see as many different types of play as possible – you can often learn as much about writing from a poorly-written play as from a well-written one. Keep your costs down by choosing the cheapest seats in midweek performances and don't forget small scale performances by touring groups and amateurs.

If possible join a local amateur dramatic group. Many well-known and successful playwrights began their careers as actors, and if you take to the stage yourself you will soon find out which plays work and which don't.

Read play scripts, these are cheap to buy and can also be borrowed from the library.

The more time you spend in the theatre world, the more you will begin to understand the needs of both the performers and the audience, and the more theatrical your scripts will become.

Good luck.

Lesley and Ann

section

one

01

a writing
mindset

In this chapter you will learn:
- about audiences
- what equipment you will
  need to write
- how to think like a writer.

The most common mistake that new playwrights make is: that new writers try to replicate something they've enjoyed and end up writing in a voice that is not their own, but a poor imitation of someone else.

Michael Jenner, writer for EastEnders, Holby, Taggart

Maybe you already have an idea for a play, and want to plunge straight into it. Fine. Get a piece of paper or open a computer file and write the idea down – that way you won't lose it and you can come back to it later, after you have done the right preparation.

On the other hand, perhaps you feel you haven't got enough imagination to be a writer. This simply isn't true. Everybody can learn to use their imagination. Think of your brain as a series of muscles – the more you use them, the stronger they get. Imagination, logic, emotional intelligence can all be improved and developed through use. Techniques such as brainstorming will help you build up your mental muscles.

The audience

A writer needs to be aware of the probable audience for the play without allowing that awareness to dictate every aspect of the play. A play that is written with the sole purpose of pleasing an audience will never be more than a trivial piece of work with no heart. A play that is written without any consideration for the audience will probably never be performed.

If you know exactly where your play is going to be performed – the school nativity for instance – then it is sensible to consider the audience quite early in the writing process. However, in most cases the best thing is to write the play that you want to write, and then decide what its audience is and how it can best reach that audience. A play can't reach its audience until a theatre company has been persuaded that it is suitable for them, so in most cases the first hurdle is to write a play that theatre people are interested in.

Practical basics

Should you use a computer, word processor, typewriter, or pen and paper? Many writers are still more comfortable with a pen and paper for early drafts and there is nothing wrong with this. It's best to create a system for organizing your work – don't let yourself be overwhelmed by scribbled piles of paper. Whether you use a loose leaf folder or an exercise book you need to keep the script under control.

Remember your script will have to be typed or printed out before you can send it off. Whether typed or computer printed, a manuscript must be immaculately presented. There is further information on script layout and presentation in Chapter 19.

There is no doubt that once you have mastered a computer or word processor many aspects of writing become much quicker and easier. You can re-write or re-organize a script, or try things out just to see how they look. Changing a character's name takes a moment, and if you don't like it you can change it back again just as easily.

Good software will help you with the layout and it is much easier to do re-writes on a computer. However, you still need to be organized. If you want to be able to refer back to earlier drafts, then you need to save each one under a different name. Remember to take backups, on floppy disc or CD, at regular intervals, and keep the backup somewhere safe away from the computer.

Top tip

However you choose to work, one essential item is a small notebook in which you can write down thoughts, ideas, snatches of dialogue, anything which could be used to good effect in your play. Carry it with you and keep it by the bed. If you lose track of the notebook, write on anything that comes to hand, but make sure you keep it safe and write it into the notebook as soon as possible. It is a truism that bears repeating often – if you don't write it down straight away it will disappear out of your mind. Forever.

Time available

You may have ambitions to become a full-time writer, but initially you will have to fit writing in with your other commitments. However you choose to do this, the main thing is to write regularly. Writing is a form of mental exercise, and the more you do it, the stronger you will become. Leaving long gaps between your writing sessions will mean that you never establish a rhythm, and each time you go back to it you will spend part of the session re-familiarizing yourself with what you wrote last time. So try to set some time aside for writing on a regular basis, even if it is only a few hours a week. For most of us it is better to write for a short time every day than for several hours once a month. If you feel you can only write at weekends, try to add one weekday evening so that you maintain the flow.

If you can't write regularly like this then don't despair, but do accept that your play will progress slowly. The danger with slow progress of course is that you may lose motivation and give up altogether without finishing the piece. You can avoid this by putting extra effort into the planning stage, so that each time you sit down to write, you only have to look at your meticulously outlined plot and detailed character studies, to know exactly what you need to do next.

Reference material

While it is not essential to have any reference books, a dictionary and a thesaurus are extremely useful. Those using a computer will already have these, but remember to set the spellchecker to UK or US English, depending on where you are sending the play. Other reference books can be acquired as needed, and writers with Internet access can use the vast online resources for research. It is always worth checking your facts, since you can be sure that there will be at least one person in an audience who will notice if you get something wrong – however obscure.

Mental basics

People watching

Drama is all about people. Even if you want to write about robots, or animals, you will find it only works if you give them human personalities. Fortunately your raw material is all around you. All the characters you will probably ever need can be found in the average high street.

Shakespeare said 'all the world's a stage' – and it is. So why not pretend that everyone around you is acting out a little play for your delight. Imagine what their lives are like. Where do they work? What relationships do they have? Spend some time alone in a crowded public place where you can watch people – a café, a railway station, or even in your car in a busy car park.

Listening

Assuming that your play is not going to be performed entirely in mime, your characters will need to communicate verbally with each other. A large part of the information given to the audience will come from speeches. So now is the time to start taking an interest in speech patterns, as well as dialects, accents, hesitation, deviation and repetition. The best way of learning about speech patterns is to listen to other people. Pay attention to how people speak and react to each other. Try to analyze why person A sounds different from person B. How do they construct their sentences? Do long words roll off their tongue in a sonorous procession, or do they use the local patois? Does the way they speak indicate their social standing and educational achievements?

It doesn't stop there though. In a play, speeches need to appear to be natural even though we all know they have been cleverly constructed, and so it is not enough to simply repeat natural speech, you will have to learn how to capture its essence.

Conversations

Pay attention to how conversations work. Without realizing it, we are all obeying the unwritten rules of conversation most of the time. Each person gets their turn to talk, and most of us understand that we have to wait our turn, and we mustn't go on for too long when we get our turn. A person who fails to observe the rules makes everyone else feel uncomfortable, and a person in crisis will probably forget the rules ever existed.

Single sex groups relate in different ways to mixed groups. It sometimes seems that women can barely function without talking to each other, whereas a group of men will work together in near silence. In a mixed group, there may be the whole business of sexual politics underlying innocent exchanges. Older people seem to get talking more easily than teenagers, who tend to eye each other up self-consciously.

Top tip

Real conversations can look very awkward on the page – try writing down a few lines from a conversation you have overheard, word for word exactly as you hear it. You'll be able to see at once how aimless and vague real speech can appear to be.

Looking

Remember that visual information is at least as important as speech in how we communicate with each other and in what we can deduce about other people.

Clothes and hair

Clothes are not just to keep us warm, dry and decent, they also are quite a good indication of a person's character, social standing, affluence and sexual availability.

Is that man in a suit an officer worker or is he someone unused to wearing formal clothing who is finding it restricting? Does that woman use clothes to conceal herself because she has low self-esteem? Is that man wearing a uniform because it gives him status? Is the girl wearing a short skirt and low cut top because she is looking for a mate?

Hair styles and bodily adornment can also reveal a lot. What do we learn about the young woman with severely pulled back hair and wearing a small crucifix? What if the crucifix was large, would that tell us something else? Is the young man with long hair unable to afford a barber or is he rebelling against society?

Body language

If clothes and hair can be an overt way of showing character then body language can be a covert way, because it is what we reveal about ourselves unconsciously. Most of us find it very difficult to control our body language and so it is often the best indicator of someone's true feelings.

Notice how people mirror each other's body language when they are in harmony – both with legs crossed say – and how they do the opposite when they are in disagreement – one with arms folded, one waving their hands about.

Imagine a scene, two lovers sitting side-by-side on a park bench staring intently into each other's eyes.

WOMAN: (*passionately*) Do you love me more than life itself?
MAN: You know I do.

Now imagine the same scene, same two lovers and same dialogue said in exactly the same way, but this time only the women is staring intently at her lover, the man is staring blankly into space. In the first case, the man's body language, in harmony with the woman's, tells us that he means what he says, but in the second case his body language, so different from the woman's, suggests he is deceiving her.

> **Top tip**
> Watching politicians is a good exercise – record a television interview and play it back in slow motion. You'll learn a lot.

Actions and social interactions

Deliberate gestures such as shaking a fist or overturning a table also reveal a lot about a person but in a much more overt and less subtle way than body language. Some people are much more animated than others, using exaggerated gestures, while others are more contained. Is the first group being melodramatic or open? And is the second group calm or repressed?

Study the way people greet each other, touch each other, leave each other and protect their personal space. Is that slap on the back a genuine sign of affection or is it an attempt to mislead the recipient into thinking that it is genuine?

Unlike body language, both actions and social interactions can be deliberately misleading.

Summary

In this chapter you have learnt:

- to understand your audience
- how to get organized
- to study other people.

02

getting started

In this chapter you will learn:
- about the basic components of a play
- how to generate ideas
- how to choose a setting.

The main thing I look for in a new script is: something I haven't read before. If the writer's voice, and their take on the world and story of the drama is authentic and consistent, and their ambition for their own writing is strong, I can be intrigued by anything.

Jessica Dromgoule, radio drama producer

Play basics

All plays have three basic components:

- setting
- plot
- characters.

Some writers start with the characters and then work out what to do with them, others have a story they want to tell, others start with a situation. There is no right or wrong way to begin.

Writers are often told to write about what they know, and this can be a good starting point as you will already have the background knowledge on the subject. If you have worked in an office you will have a good understanding of office politics. On the other hand, unless you are in close touch with teenagers it can be difficult for the older writer to write authoritatively on youth culture.

Top tip

If you choose to write about something outside your personal experience, then you will need to do some serious research, and more importantly, you will need to find some aspect of your chosen area that resonates with you personally. If, for instance, you come from a Welsh mining family, you might feel you can write about workers in a South African diamond mine. If you don't have some sort of connection, however loose, your play will lack passion.

Generating ideas

The initial idea for a play can come from anywhere. Watching dandelion seeds drift through your garden can set you thinking about the randomness of life, overhearing a bizarre snatch of conversation on a bus can give you the germ of a plot, reading an autobiography can give you a character. The finished play may be true to the original idea or may have completely lost sight of it – that really doesn't matter.

You may be daunted at the thought of generating ideas, but after a while you will develop a habit of seeing dramatic potential all around you. There are some tricks of the trade that may help.

- **Daydreaming.** Daydreaming is extremely useful – lie back, close your eyes, and let your mind wander. After a few minutes, write down whatever you were thinking about. It won't in itself be a play, but it may be the germ of an idea.
- **Brainstorming.** Choose a topic and write down whatever springs to mind around that topic. Take a large piece of paper – a piece torn from cheap lining paper for walls is ideal. Choose a topic and write it in the middle of the paper. Draw a circle round it, then draw lines radiating out. At the end of each line, put any associated words that come to mind, each in their own circle. Look at each associated word and surround it with its own set of associations. Keep going – you'll be surprised where it leads you.
- **Your family.** Look at your own family, both past and present. Some of the best dramas are based on the minutiae of family life. Either use an actual event and write a play about it, or let it be a starting point for a fictional drama. For instance, John Mortimer used his childhood as source material for *A Voyage Around My Father* which has been a book, a television play and a stage play. However, take care that you are not belittling or libelling anyone. Even if you are writing about members of your own family they could still sue you.
- **Local stories and media articles.** Newspapers, particularly local ones, are full of potential dramas. Choose an article at random and see if you can create a play from it. Surfing the net can also throw up endless possibilities.
- **Traditional stories.** Look at traditional stories and the work of other writers. Shakespeare took many of his plots from other works and in turn his plays have provided inspiration to other writers. It isn't plagiarism if you use a play, book or film as an inspiration and write a sequel, a prequel or a modern version. Fables, fairy tales and Greek myths can also be given a modern twist. The original inspiration for *Pygmalion* by George Bernard Shaw was the Greek myth of Pygmalion. We took the same idea and turned it into our own comedy, *Living Doll*.

- **Music.** Music can give inspiration. Play a piece of music and write down what it conjures up. Or take popular songs and create a story from their lyrics.
- **Paintings.** Paintings may provide a starting point. What kind of lives did the subjects lead? Some research into a picture, or the artist, could trigger thoughts for a drama.

Ideas unleashed

Once you become alive to the potential drama all around you there won't be a shortage of plays in your mind – the problem will be choosing which one to write first. At this stage you will need to develop another skill – learning to select the ideas that have got the potential for development.

Although ideas can come from almost anything, most writing is sparked by thinking about characters or situations. There is no golden rule about which comes first, just do whatever works for you. Both character and situation are equally important. The character is only interesting if you put him or her into a situation. The situation is only interesting if it causes people to reveal their character through their reaction to it. Each time you change the combination of character and situation, you can see a completely different set of dramatic potentials.

Settings

Where are people forced to interact?

Drama arises out of the interactions between people (although the 'person' can be a robot, an animal, or anything else to which we can assign a personality). One of the most challenging forms for writer, actor and audience is probably the monologue. What, inevitably, does the character talk about? The interaction between themselves and other people, of course.

Even in a monologue, the setting matters. Is the character waiting for someone or something? Are they at home? Or stuck in a lift? The setting will affect their mood, the things they tell the audience, and what is revealed about them. So you need to think about where to set your play, and for anything other than a monologue, look for situations where people are forced to interact.

Types of setting

Hospitals make great settings since medical matters are a natural source of drama, and because most of the people in them can't get out for one reason or another. Families, work places, public transport, restaurants, hotels, cinemas, theatres, airplanes, World War One slit trenches, are all examples of situations where people are obliged to interact and can't get away. Even a queue creates a small setting for a drama. In fact, the more trapped people are the more they are forced to interact, which is why the principle of claustrophobia is important in drama.

Exercise 1

Make a list of at least ten places where people are forced to interact.

The principle of claustrophobia

Imagine a situation where two people start a conversation that quickly turns into an argument. One of them gets so angry they get up and leave, never to return. That is the end of that character's involvement in whatever drama ensues. But, supposing those two people work in the same office and neither can afford to walk out of their job, the drama between them will be ongoing. That is the principle of claustrophobia.

There are degrees of claustrophobia – it is much easier to walk away from an evening at the cinema than from Christmas dinner with your family. The strongest dramas are usually in the most claustrophobic settings. Bear in mind that claustrophobia can be emotional as well as physical – it's the emotional pressure that stops someone walking away from the Christmas dinner, and that is extremely powerful.

Open and closed environments

When you are trying to assess a setting for a play, consider whether in real life the environment is open or closed. An open environment is something like a shop, where anybody can come and go as they choose. An example of a closed environment would be a Managing Director's office, where very few people would be admitted. The more closed the environment, the more claustrophobic it is likely to be, but also the fewer reasons people might have to enter or leave the environment.

You can use either type of environment as a setting, but you need to understand the implications for your play. If a setting is very closed, you will have a static but more intense play – because a closed setting is inherently more claustrophobic. Closed settings are often easier to create in the practical sense – an office or a living room can be set quite realistically and simply whereas a supermarket or a forest takes a bit more thought. On the other hand an open setting allows a greater range of characters to interact.

Consider the hospital setting. People in a queue there would probably be in a large open reception area, with a receptionist behind a desk and other people moving through the area as they go about their business. Lots of potential for interaction, but probably easier to do on television or film.

On the other hand, the consultant's office in the hospital is a much more closed setting and easier to create, but what is going to happen in there? He or she will see a patient, then another, maybe talk to the nurse in between patients. There will be only one door, a telephone, a computer. This is fine if you want to write a close study of, say, how the consultant breaks bad news to a patient, not so good if you're aiming for a comedy with multiple complications.

The waiting area in a hospital clinic on the other hand provides a good compromise. It is reasonably closed and claustrophobic because the people waiting are trapped by the system – they have to wait for their turn to see the consultant. It is open enough to give a wide range of characters, so that a cleaner might be sitting next to a teacher, and both with the same health problem.

If you are using more than one set you can achieve contrast, say between the closed world of the consultant's office and the more open environment of the waiting room.

Exercise 2

Go through the list from Exercise 1 and decide how claustrophobic each setting is, and how open or closed.

Work in progress

We devised a list that included:

- waiting for the Post Office to open
- a coach party in a café taking up more than one table
- an office.

The conversation outside the Post Office takes place in an open situation. All the people can walk away from each other. The conversation in the café takes place in a closed situation. Although any of the people could walk out, because they are part of a party which has to stay together, this scene has more dramatic potential than the previous one. The conversation in the office takes place in a closed situation, but it is more claustrophobic than the café – the people are forced to stay and interact with each other, otherwise they could be out of a job.

Summary

In this chapter you have learnt:

- how to work with the basic components of a play
- how to generate ideas through various techniques
- how to choose a setting that allows interaction between characters.

03

creating and working with characters

In this chapter you will learn:
- how to find sources for characters
- about aspects of character creation
- about types of character.

The main thing I look for in a new script is: do I believe in the characters, do I care about them and do I sympathize with what they are hoping to achieve.

Ray Cooney, playwright

As we showed in Chapter 02, the basic idea for a play can come from almost anything. There are no rules for how you develop the idea either, but at some point you will have to think about the characters, and for most writers that point comes sooner rather than later. Sometimes it won't need any thought, and the characters will occur to you as part of the basic play idea. But don't worry if that doesn't happen. Inspiration is only a very small part of writing, and if you have to construct your characters cold-bloodedly it won't matter. An audience won't be interested in how you arrived at your play, they will only judge you on what they experience during the performance.

Initially you should expect to spend equal amounts of time on developing all your characters. You need to get to know them, understand them and create a background and a life story for them. But for most of the characters very little of this will find its way into the finished play, because they are not important enough to warrant it. However, your detailed knowledge and understanding of each character will add to the richness of the play and feed through into your writing as subtext. (For a definition of subtext see p. 27.)

Sources for characters

You can generate characters in the same ways as you generate ideas for plays – daydream, brainstorm, look around you, read books and so on. The sources for your characters are all around you.

- **Strangers**. This is where the time spent people watching pays off. You should already have a collection of interesting but briefly observed characters ready for fleshing out.
- **Family and friends**. Most of the characters we create are fictional, but one simple trick is to look at people you already know. It's not a question of replicating them, but of picking up on certain aspects of their character to get you started. So, even if you begin with Great Uncle Charlie it is unlikely that the character will eventually be recognizable as him, because in the process of writing you will incorporate characteristics which Great Uncle Charlie doesn't have.

- **Stock characters.** The bossy mother-in-law, forgetful professor, sullen teenager, tart with a heart etc. can all make good starting points but it is important to give them other characteristics so that they move away from being a one-dimensional stereotype. See below for more on how to use stock characters.

- **Plays, films, television and novels.** These days we are surrounded by fictional characters. Without realizing it, we are constantly absorbing the work of other writers, and inevitably when we create our own characters something of that appears in our work. There is no crime in consciously looking at other fictional characters and picking up on anything that resonates for you.

- **Real life.** If your play is about a well-known person or a historical figure then you will have your characters ready-made. You will have read around the subject, you will know about their friends, family and colleagues, and you will have your own opinion about them. The play will be your creative interpretation of that person's life, and while you may have to alter timescales, or combine several people into one supporting character, you will be aiming to convey the emotional and psychological truths about that person.

Top tip

Try taking a character from an old novel or play, such as Heathcliff from *Wuthering Heights* or Lady Macbeth from *Macbeth*, then re-create them for the modern world. Keep their character the same as the original and imagine that character moved into the twenty-first century.

Exercise 3

Make a list of at least ten characters, taken from a range of sources. Keep the description of each one brief at this stage.

Aspects of character creation

Character and characterization

Characterization is the surface of a human being, their appearance, movements and outward behaviour. Character is what lies deeper.

A writer needs to think about each character's background, and endeavour to understand what makes them tick. Was there something in their childhood, or is it the trials and tribulations of adult life that have formed them? It's probably true that the earlier a character trait is formed, the deeper it goes and the harder it is for the person to change it, so it is those early influences that are most interesting to the writer

Stock characters

Stock characters, such as those listed above, are predictable, and behave in ways that the audience expects. They have their uses, especially in minor roles because the audience already knows all about this type of character, so the writer does not have to spend time explaining them. If every single character you create is startlingly original you may simply end up with confusion. However, stage plays on the whole have small casts, and the characters have to interact intensively with each other, so there are few uses for completely stock characters. On the other hand, the writer can manipulate the audience's perceptions of these stereotypes. When a character first appears, we must expect the audience to make certain deductions based on their initial behaviour, and the most likely deductions will be based on cliché.

You now have a range of choices as to what to do with this character. You can stick with the stereotype and allow the character to become more and more monstrous. This works in comedy, because an audience's expectations will have limits, and overstepping those limits will lead to laughter. In a serious play you can still go to extremes, or you can look for the contrasts that lie beneath the character's façade.

Revealing character traits

There is a difference between hidden character traits and traits that appear as a result of the conflict and pressure in the play. Hidden character traits which were always there should emerge naturally as part of the process of revealing the character. Traits that appear as a result of the events in the play are the most important of all, and should be shown as dramatically as possible.

Case study: traits that emerge during the play

In *Sleuth* by Anthony Shaffer the first act consists of an elaborate and deeply unpleasant trick that Andrew Wyke plays on Milo Tindle, a rather repressed and overly polite young man. Milo is convinced that Andrew is going to kill him, and is so terrified that he faints when a gun is fired, although it is only a blank. In Act II we meet a different Milo. Facing death has changed him, so that he can cold-bloodedly exact his revenge on Andrew, something that the Milo of Act I would never have done.

Character contrasts

It is possible to imagine a story with characters who are all very similar to each other, but it is very hard to see where the interest in such a story would lie. If everybody agrees about everything, there is no conflict, and conflict is the lifeblood of drama.

Once you have created your main character, you need to think about setting up other characters in contrast to them. This can be a real difficulty for beginners, since a writer's first efforts are often based on their own experience.

Top tip

If you write a play about your adolescence, and a reader complains that the main character and their best friend are too similar too each other, don't reply 'but that's how it was in real life.' Create a new best friend, one that offers a contrast to the main character and watch your story come to life.

Exercise 4

Examine your list of characters and put them into contrasted pairs.

Social and cultural background

This is where the common exhortation to 'write what you know' comes into its own, especially in your first play. Whether you are middle class or working class, BA Oxon or BA

University of Life, you have special and detailed knowledge of at least one area of our life and culture. Use it.

Willy Russell, for instance, has made extensive use of his Liverpool background in plays such as *Educating Rita* and *Shirley Valentine*.

Exercise 5

From your list of characters take the pair that is the most sharply contrasted and describe their social and cultural backgrounds. They will be the two most important characters in your scene.

Characters' names

Names carry a lot of significance and your choice of names for your characters can have profound implications for your play. Samuel Beckett asserted consistently that his unseen character Godot was not named and did not stand for God, but to his apparent irritation commentators have regularly suggested that was the case.

Names say something about the age, class and nationality of a character. The rules of cliché apply here, and as usual they can work both for you and against you. An audience will assume that any character called Kylie will probably have been born in the 1980s and without a silver spoon in their mouth, or that a Gertrude was born before the Second World War. Names like this can be used to quickly convey information about a character, but if they are too obviously clichéd they can predispose the audience to decide against your play before the curtains even open, while they are reading the cast list in the programme. On the other hand you can work against the cliché, so that your Kylie grows up to be a high flying career girl who hides her name behind an enigmatic initial, or your Gertrude is a young fashionable woman named after her Great Aunt.

Names of course all have histories and meanings, and it is worth knowing what these are. Kylie is alleged to be an aborigine word for boomerang, whereas Gertrude is Germanic and means 'strong spear'. These meanings could be used to underline or contrast the characters that bear the names. While few people will be consciously aware of these meanings, they still add another layer of significance to your text.

Names also carry cultural significance. It is many years since Winston Churchill died but calling a character Winston will instantly associate him with Churchill in some way.

Names can be used to indicate a character's temperament. Someone called Jim sounds as if he would be an honest reliable citizen while Marigold sounds as if she would be flighty.

Once you have named your characters remember that other characters may well use shortened versions, nicknames and endearments, all of which can be used to infer the nature of their relationship and the current state of play between them.

Don't forget surnames. It may seem far too obvious to call a murderer Mr Carver or a lover Mr Heart, but in fact many writers use surnames to underline characteristics. Sometimes just changing the spelling – Karver or Hart – is enough to take the edge off the obviousness while still retaining an echo of the meaning. In *Death of a Salesman* Arthur Miller called his salesman Loman – (Low-man) as a straightforward way of indicating the man's true status.

Case study: names

In our comedy, *Whatever You Want*, Margaret calls her husband Ray some of the time, but mostly she calls him Raymond, a sure sign that he is in trouble. And Dilys' name was chosen purely because of the assonance with silly.

Exercise 6

Choose names for all your characters.

Physical attributes

If you have followed the advice in Chapter 01 and studied real people you will now find it easy to develop a strong idea of each character's physical attributes: how they look, how they dress, how they move. This will be invaluable in the early stages of writing. You will be able to visualize each scene and walk through it in your mind. The characters will live for you. You can put all this information into early drafts of the script, but most of it will have to come out before the script is submitted – detailed descriptions make casting too difficult.

Motivation and psychology

Motivation operates at many levels. Thirst will motivate someone to want a drink; fear of failure, instilled in childhood, will motivate someone to drive themselves beyond breaking point. The most superficial motivations can be used to move a plot forward. If you need a character to leave the stage, by all means have them complain of thirst and exit to the kitchen to make tea, but be sure you integrate this fully into the story of the play.

Within each character there will be at least two levels of motivation. The most obvious is what hits the audience first, and beneath the obvious motivation is something even deeper. Most of us are not even aware of what drives us in life – which is why therapy is such a fast-growing industry. Similarly your characters don't have to be aware of their deep motivations – but the writer needs to know exactly what is going on. Unlike stereotype, where even the deep motivation is predictable, you need to create characters whose deep motivations are both unexpected and realistic.

Some writers think of this deep motivation as a character's secret, and although they know what it is they never make it apparent, even to the audience. That way the character has an internal logic and becomes far more realistic. The internal logic doesn't need to be made explicit, because we rarely find out about the deepest motivations of other people, but their choices are underpinned by it.

Case study: motivation

When we first meet Margaret in *Whatever You Want*, her most obvious motivation is a desire to better herself materially – she appears to want the business to succeed so that she can have more status in the community, a nicer house and fancy holidays. She is so focused on this that she is not at all sympathetic to her old friend Dilys, who is heartbroken because her marriage has broken up.

We learn gradually that Margaret's deep motivation goes back to school days, when Dilys was a pretty girl and Margaret was her plain, overweight sidekick. Ever since then she has been re-inventing herself until she is now thin and well-groomed, in contrast to Dilys, who has let herself go.

You don't need a degree in the subject of psychology to have an insight into psychological makeup. Your own personal view of the world will colour everything you write and your beliefs about people, and your insights into their makeup, will be crucial in giving your work its unique voice.

Once you have created your characters you will need to inhabit their world as you write, so that each reaction and response is true to the character and not just put in to move the plot along or provide a cue for another character. This cannot be stressed too highly. If you manipulate your characters like puppets the audience will pick up on it and nothing will irritate them more than when they see someone acting completely out of character for no good reason.

Vices and virtues

In early forms of drama, such as the medieval Morality Play, characters were simple representations of one virtue or vice, such as Envy, Lust, Justice and Mercy. Now we look for more complicated and realistic representations of human beings in our drama. All of your main characters should have both virtue and vice, light and shade. Secondary characters however can be more one-dimensional, and can be used to embody one particular virtue or vice.

Exercise 7

Returning to the most contrasted pair of characters, decide on each one's basic psychology, their vices and virtues, and their motivation.

Binding ties and what's at stake

Characters also need a good reason to stay in a situation which is causing them pain or anguish, otherwise they would just walk away and that would be the end of the play. Binding ties, in other words, are the character-based aspect of claustrophobia. Always ask yourself the questions 'why do characters stay?' and 'what is in it for them?'

Some of the answers will be down to the claustrophobia of the setting – if your characters are stuck in a lift then they have to stay, and the interest in the play will arise out of how they behave when they are trapped in this way. But what about characters who are not so obviously trapped? What keeps Felix and Oscar together in Neil Simon's play *The Odd Couple*? The answer has to arise out of each character's psychology and emotional needs. So, this is another type of conflict, caused by the psychological quirk that we often need the very people who drive us to distraction. This explains the enduring fascination for writers of the unhappy marriage (*Cat On A Hot Tin Roof*, *Who's Afraid of Virginia Woolf?* and so on). A couple who are destroying each other stay together for all sorts of reasons – economic, social, family – but if deep down they also need each other then that will be the most binding tie of all.

Case study: binding ties

In *Whatever You Want* Ray wants to retire to a little bungalow by the sea and Margaret doesn't. What stops Ray leaving Margaret? They are married and they have financial ties which make it difficult for him to walk away. But what really holds him to her is that he can't cope on his own and he doesn't want to be on his own in retirement.

Characters also remain in a situation if there is something to be gained from staying. Money is a strong motivating force. A possible inheritance could keep a niece tied to a demanding aunt. Similarly, a roof over her head can keep a woman in an unhappy marriage.

Case study: what's at stake?

In our play *Ashes to Ashes* the characters are bound to each other by murder. If either left, the murder would be revealed.

Conflict in character

Once you understand a character's motivation and binding ties, you will see where their conflict originates. The plot of your play will place them in conflict with the world around them, but there will also be inner conflict between their obvious motivation and their deeper motivation. Conflict is another way in which character and plot are interwoven. Your characters need to be in conflict with both themselves (character) and the world around them (plot). For more about this, see Chapter 07.

Case study: inner conflict

In Margaret's case (in *Whatever you Want*), no amount of material success will compensate her for the pain of rejection when she was young. And she is reminded of that every day in the form of her husband Ray, whom she married in desperation because she felt nobody else would have her. Her drive to make money is in conflict with her need to be loved.

Exercise 8

Decide what binding ties, if any, exist between your two characters, and what might be at stake for them. If your instinct is telling you at this stage that they are strangers, then concentrate on each one individually, and decide what their inner conflicts are.

Subtext

Subtext is all the things that are going on under the surface of the play. It is not what a character says, but what they don't say, or what they say unintentionally. It develops gradually through the course of the play to give a picture of the deep motivations of the characters and the essential truth that is driving the plot. The underlying conflict in the drama will come across in the subtext.

It is easiest to spot in real life with people you know well. If a family member hits their head and keeps saying that they feel fine, you will know, apparently instinctively, if they aren't fine at all. Because you know them well you will recognize the subtext in their statement.

This is why you need to know your characters inside out. Once you do, a lot of subtext will appear without you needing to create it deliberately. However, if you have a scene where subtext is particularly important, there are various ways to achieve it.

- **Contradictory body language.** Have a character say one thing while their actions are indicating something completely different. Body language is often a giveaway. If someone is deliberately concealing something they will be careful what they say, but probably less careful about their body language. Or, if two people are in an argument that looks like turning into a fist fight, their body language will indicate how likely that is – people who don't really want to fight tend to back off, even while saying aggressive words. Superficially the relationship may look confrontational, but the subtext is saying something quite different.

- **Decoy technique.** Have a character talking about a third person when it is obvious they are really talking about themselves.
- **Protesting too much.** Have a character express such strongly held views on a subject that the audience comes to suspect they may be feeling the opposite. For example a character who is a rampant homophobe, may be hiding, or refusing to face up to, their own homosexual tendencies. The high flying career woman who says she despises marriage, or the childless woman who says she has never wanted children, could both be hiding a deep biological need. They are all protesting too much.
- **Clothes.** Use the character's dress to say something about them. A shy girl who says she isn't interested in boys, but is wearing a fitted satin blouse, is subconsciously inviting a man to notice her.
- **Freudian slips.** This is when a character unintentionally says the wrong word and in fact says a word that reveals what they are really thinking. Remember to use this sparingly.

In addition, subtext is also generated by characters' names, use of props, lighting effects and so on.

The writer is dependant on the actor getting the subtext across to the audience and that is what they are trained to do. As long as you know and understand the subtext behind your dialogue, it will come out in the writing.

Generally speaking subtext should be subtle, audiences are quite sensitive to it and will pick up on the slightest nuance. If it is heavily signposted it won't work, and you may even find yourself generating unintentional laughter. In true comedy of course it can be laid on with a trowel. A character struggling around with both arms and legs in plaster, all the while insisting that they are absolutely fine, makes us laugh even though we know they are suffering horribly.

Character categories

Protagonist

Everyone is the hero of their own life. The most common way to tell a story is to follow the fortunes of one main character. This central protagonist is surrounded by lesser characters, whose lives are subordinated to theirs and who are clearly not heroes. There is a simple reason for this apparent anomaly – audience identification. Precisely because we all tend to see ourselves as centre stage in our own life we find it easiest to engage with one central protagonist.

We say 'protagonist' instead of 'hero' or 'heroine' because, clearly, the central character doesn't have to be heroic. There is a long tradition of placing rogues and crooks at the centre of a story, and a more recent tradition of the anti-hero. This is fine, as long as there is something in the character for the audience to connect with. This doesn't mean they have to be lovable, especially in the theatre where the audience is often more willing to engage intellectually than the audience for, say, film and television. You can write a play about a psychopathic mass murderer, and although it is unlikely to be a popular hit, it may well find a niche audience.

Sometimes plays have two central characters, rather like the buddy movie format. They both need to be strong characters and of course they should be opposed in some way. In *The Odd Couple* tidy Felix and slobbish Oscar are perfectly opposed.

Exercise 9

Decide if one of your pair of characters is strong enough to be the protagonist, or if you see them as equally important.

Narrator

A narrator can be used to guide the audience through the play. They can be a character in the play, or stand completely outside it. Brian Friel's *Dancing At Lughnasa* uses the character of Michael as the narrator, looking back as an adult on events in his childhood. The narrator provides another type of texture to a play, crossing the divide between the audience and the play by talking directly to the audience and drawing them in.

The danger of using a narrator is that a writer can easily become lazy and use the narration to solve script problems, or allow the narrator to ramble on for too long. Write the narration as if it were a poem or a short story, both forms in which every word has to count.

Other major characters

Inevitably, as you construct your plot, one or more characters will come to feel nearly as important as the protagonist. They become important by virtue of their function in the plot and their relationship to the protagonist. Their story can be used to reinforce, reflect, underline or counterpoint the protagonist's story. The most important of these characters will need to be just as carefully drawn as the protagonist. Secondary characters are usually in strong contrast to the protagonist but are sometimes a weaker version of them. Where the protagonist might be willing to commit murder to achieve their ends, their sidekick might pull back at the last moment.

In a play with two protagonists there can be another pair, of lesser importance, whose story runs alongside that of the main two. In *The Importance of Being Ernest,* Oscar Wilde interweaves the main plot of John and Gwendolyn with that of Algernon and Cecily. Similarly in the musical *Guys and Dolls,* the central love story of Sky Masterson and Sarah Brown is paralleled with the story of Nathan Detroit and Miss Adelaide.

Somebody to talk to

Don Quixote had his Sancho Panza, Batman has Robin – if you have one central protagonist then they will need a way to share their thoughts with the audience. One solution is to give them a companion. It doesn't have to be a positive relationship – there can be more mileage in antagonism. Imagine a vicar stuck in a lift with his churchwarden – you could make a two-handed play out of that. Now imagine the vicar trapped with an atheist – wouldn't that make an even better play?

The important thing is to give the protagonist a reason for confiding in the other character, whether it's a commonality of purpose or just plain loneliness.

Minor characters

If you throw a stone into a pond the ripples move outward from the centre. The protagonist is the stone at the centre, and the secondary characters are ranged along the ripples in varying degrees of importance. The ripples on the far edges are small but still an important part of the overall pattern.

Minor characters are like those tiny ripples. They need to be just as carefully thought through as major characters, otherwise they won't come to life, although very little of their development will be revealed in the play. In fact if they are drawn in too much detail they will distract the audience's attention from the main characters.

Work in progress

Our list includes two working women of different ages, two elderly women of different temperaments, and two young men, one who likes sport and one who doesn't.

The two women of different ages are Beryl and Mel, the two elderly women are Iris and Pam, the two young men are Steve, who likes sport, and Gary, who doesn't. Beryl and Mel are the most sharply contrasted pair, so we have chosen them.

Beryl is in her middle fifties. She is married and has children who have left home. She is good at her job, very efficient, doesn't suffer fools gladly and can be bossy. Underneath this, though, she desperately wants to be liked, and bossy people are often not liked. Mel is in her late teens or early twenties. She still lives at home and enjoys clubbing. Underneath her modern, brittle surface, she is basically a kind girl who raises money for animal charities. She is not as efficient as Beryl at her job, but she is better with modern technology. Because she is open and friendly she is liked by everyone, even if they have to work a bit harder because of her errors.

What are the binding ties holding the two women to their jobs? Beryl needs to keep her job, perhaps because her husband is out of work or doesn't earn enough. Mel is not quite so bothered about keeping her job for financial reasons, but she fancies someone in another department. If we decide that they both work in the same office, then the ties that keep them to their jobs will also oblige them to get along together. Both have something at stake in the work situation – loss of money for Beryl and loss of a romantic opportunity for Mel. Beryl is in conflict with her boss, with her work, with Mel and with herself – she doesn't like herself. Mel has far less conflict, as long as she can get her man she is happy. Because of this, Beryl is going to be the protagonist.

Summary

In this chapter you have learnt:

- how to find characters in real life and in fiction
- how to understand the various types of character
- to appreciate the use of stock characters
- to look for contrasts
- to understand the motivation of characters.

04

speech and dialogue

In this chapter you will learn:
- about speech
- about dialogue.

The main thing I look for in a new script is: an original voice and a genuine desire to tell that particular story.

**Michael Jenner, writer for EastEnders,
Holby City, Taggart**

Speech

Speech patterns

If you have done the listening task in Chapter 01 you will already have an understanding of the qualities of natural speech. Each of us has a unique way of speaking, which is an amalgam of all the external influences we've been exposed to, filtered through our own nature and personality. Your characters need the same rich mix in their speech.

You should start by establishing how your protagonist speaks. The other characters' speech patterns will either reflect or contrast with the protagonist. It is essential to give each character their own speech pattern. It should be possible to look at a script and recognize who each speaker is from the way they talk rather than by looking at the character names. Script readers will often cover the names on the left hand side of the page and read a few speeches to see if they can distinguish the speakers, and if they can't that constitutes a big black mark against that script.

You may choose to design a play where many of the characters have the same speech pattern. Robots, for instance, would all talk the same, except the rogue robot that is different from the others in some way. Only let this happen deliberately, never accidentally.

The degree to which speech appears natural depends on the character and the moment in which they find themselves. It also depends on the type of play. A historical drama could have quite stylized speeches while a modern take on life could be full of slang and bad grammar.

Accents and dialects

Accents are to do with the way words are pronounced in different regions and by different social classes of people. They can tell us a great deal about a person because they indicate where they come from, their social standing and their education. Also accent is a speech characteristic that varies according to situation. A character might start off with a standard English accent and under pressure slip into broad cockney – suddenly we realize they are not what they appear to be. We have all met the person whose accent suddenly disappears when they are trying to impress, and many of us have a special voice for the phone.

Your choice of accent will depend primarily on where your play is set. If it is based in the Liverpool docks then all your characters could well have Liverpool accents. Beware of adding accents just as a form of decoration. Remember that by specifying an accent you are adding to the difficulties of casting – some actors can reproduce almost any accent, while others have very limited skills.

Do not try to reproduce accent phonetically throughout the script, as that can be very irritating to the reader – just say at the head of the script what accent the characters should have.

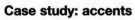

Case study: accents

In *Whatever You Want* we had three different accents, which generated laughs but which were also there for a reason. Steve and Dilys still spoke with their native Somerset accent, whereas Margaret, coming from the same background, had tried to lose hers as a way of being upwardly mobile. Her husband Ray had a strong Birmingham accent. Margaret had scorned the local boys and married Ray because she thought that as a city boy he would be going places. She was wrong, and Ray's quick fire speech pattern belies his fundamentally lazy nature.

If accents are largely about pronunciation, dialects are concerned with grammar and vocabulary. They add another layer of colour, but again try to avoid phonetically spelling words in dialect – it is difficult to read. Indicate dialect by using one or two common phrases from that particular region. For example a Bristolian might say: 'Where's he to then?' instead of 'Where is he?' A slight rearrangement of words in a sentence is often all that is needed to indicate the vernacular.

Unless you are writing for a very tightly defined audience you should avoid extreme forms of dialect because they simply won't be accessible to many people. Don't use any dialect that you are not familiar with, the chances of getting it right are minimal.

Case study: writing dialect

Here is an example of how we represented Dilys' speech in *Whatever You Want*:

DILYS: But my heart is broken! I can't go on a diet when I's pining! I wants my Steve back. I wants his strong manly arms to enfold us and clutch us to his chest…

It shows the grammar of her Somerset speech which gives both the reader and the actor a feel for what's needed. An attempt to render it phonetically would also have made it difficult to read:

DILYS:	But me 'eart's broken! I can't go on a diyet when I's piyning! I wants me Steve back. I wants 'is strong manly arrrms to enfold us and clutch us ter 'is chest...

Mummerset

Mummerset is what actors call a generalized rustic accent that could place the character in any of Britain's country areas. There are other equivalents – an all-purpose northern accent that could be Yorkshire or Lancashire, a drama school cockney that no real Londoner ever used, and so on. It's easy to dismiss these as fake, but in fact they have their uses, mainly because audiences recognize them instantly. The basic rule is that the further you are from the real thing, the more you can use the generic version. Don't insult a Yorkshire audience with a vaguely northern character, but you may have more leeway with American or European accents.

Hesitation, deviation and repetition

Ordinary speech is full of these. The trick of writing convincing dialogue is to make the speech appear natural while removing all the irritating and unnecessary parts. Only put these in where they are essential to the moment.

Case study: using hesitation

Here is Ray in *Whatever You Want* making a phone call very reluctantly:

RAY: Yes alright. Er, the thing is, Steve, it's, er, about Dilys. She asked me to phone you, I'm not quite sure why...

Most of the time his speech is direct and to the point, so that these sudden hesitations clearly show that he is struggling.

Silence between speeches is indicated by the stage direction *pause*. Within a speech it can be *pause* or *beat*. A pause is longer than a beat and can be used to indicate that a character has had a sudden thought, or has realized they are saying something they shouldn't, or has realized something about a previous speech or event. A beat is the merest hesitation and is used a lot in comedy to time a laugh.

Vocabulary

Another aspect of speech that is revealed by careful listening is the differences in vocabulary. One person says 'stomach ache', another says 'gut-rot', and both of them if talking to a child, would probably say 'pain in your tummy'. Each of your characters needs their own vocabulary, which, once established, can be modified in response to other characters.

Tongue twisters

Don't let this happen accidentally, it's not fair to put actors through torture without good reason. A good way to avoid unintentional tongue twisters is to read your script aloud – even better, listen while someone else reads it to you.

Exercise 10

Make brief notes about the speech patterns of your two characters. For each one, decide if they speak quickly or slowly, confidently or hesitantly, with or without an accent. Try speaking out loud as if you were the character.

Monologue

Writing monologues is a real challenge. You have only one character, who is engaged in a dialogue with themselves. Through their voice you have to tell a story and reveal their character. The main convention of monologue is that the speaker is confiding in some unseen listener. Sometimes we are aware who that is – a psychiatrist for instance. In other monologues the speaker addresses the audience directly but rarely as if they were an audience in a theatre.

Another convention is that the speaker has their public face on, and is presenting themselves in what they believe to be a good light. In other words, the dramatic monologue is not usually an interior monologue in the way that it sometimes is in a novel. For this reason, the hardest thing is to show the audience an aspect of character that the speaker is unaware of. If you can manage that, the audience will be gripped.

It is easy to show the surface of a character, but that won't be very interesting for an audience. You need to reveal deeper character. One way of doing this is through the stories the character tells, and the way in which they tell them. It's harder by far to show negative aspects of character, the sort of thing people don't want anyone to know about. Fortunately we all have a habit of self-justification, and that can be used to great effect.

To see truly subtle monologues, go to a performance of Alan Bennett's *Talking Heads*. (They're also available on DVD or as books.)

Top tip

Before you start on a play, writing a monologue for the main characters is a good way of establishing their ways of speaking. It helps you develop the character to the point where you really feel you know them well.

Exercise 11

Write short monologues for each of your two main characters explaining why they are unavoidably late for an appointment with a doctor. Now re-write them explaining why they are late for Christmas dinner with the family.

Two things should be immediately obvious from this exercise. Firstly, it is very difficult to capture a speech pattern of a real person. This isn't about exactly reproducing their speech, which we already know would be tedious for an audience to sit through, it is about capturing the flavour of the way they talk, and what it tells you about their personality. Secondly, almost everybody talks to their doctor quite differently from how they talk to their family. Their speech is not only affected by their personality, but by the situation they find themselves in. And suppose they were not unavoidably late, but were late through their own laziness or inefficiency – the speeches would be different again.

When you are writing for an invented character, you need to bear all of these things in mind. Not only will their speech be affected by their personality, situation and mood, but they will be constantly reacting to the other characters in the scene, who are all also affected by their own personality, situation, mood and by other characters. Don't be daunted, however. At any one point in a play, a character's speech will have one main purpose, and the other functions will be less important. Also, once you know your characters really well you will be able to write in their voice quite naturally.

Dialogue

As soon as you have two characters speaking, you have dialogue. Even if they are talking at cross purposes, or not listening to each other, it is still dialogue. Dialogue fulfils several functions in a play.

- **Giving information.** This is the simplest task of dialogue, but not the easiest to carry off successfully. Nobody likes to see the strings on a puppet, or the sweat on a ballerina, and your audience will not enjoy dialogue that is an obvious plot device. Information has to be slipped into a dialogue that is apparently about something else.
- **Moving the plot forward.** The main drivers of plot tend to be actions, or events – a new character entering, an accident, a phone call. Sometimes the event arises out of the dialogue, for instance when one character says something that upsets another, or when a character reveals a secret to another. Try to avoid moving your plot forward through dialogue that has no dramatic impact however.
- **Revealing character.** In life most conversation is superficial, and although everything we say will reveal our character, it's likely to be a slow process and of very little interest to most of the people we speak to. On the stage every word has to count. Even the most trivial exchange should be in character and add to the audience's understanding of your characters and their relationships.

Case study: revealing character

Here are Margaret and Dilys from *Whatever You Want* doing their makeup:

DILYS: *(big sigh)* It's like old times, innit Marg? Remember, when us was getting ready to go out? We both used to squash into the bathroom, sharing all our makeup and stuff.

(Dilys pokes about in Margaret's vanity case.)

MARGARET: As I recall it, you never had any makeup, you used to help yourself to mine.

DILYS: I never.

MARGARET: Well you are now. Put that blusher back.

The topic is trivial enough, but we learn that Dilys is a dreamer, wallowing in nostalgia, while Margaret's memories are quite different, and we also learn that at this point in the play Margaret is assuming dominance over Dilys.

Refining dialogue

Tempo

If you find that your dialogue is all moving at the same speed, you have a problem – your drama isn't very dramatic. Inevitably, people speak faster at moments of crisis – unless of course they are speechless with shock or horror. Each character will have their own natural tempo – forceful characters such as Margaret will tend to speak quickly in short sentences. This can be emphasized by having the other characters speak more slowly – which is what we did with Dilys. Or, if your protagonist is a downtrodden young woman, she should speak slowly and hesitantly while the other characters speak more fluently and confidently.

There will also be a tempo in the actual exchanges between characters. An argument moves quickly, a love scene more slowly. A fast-moving dialogue will need short, simple words that are easy for an actor to say.

Speech length

It is best to keep most speeches short – not more than three lines, and preferably shorter. This is particularly true if the play is moving towards a climax. This makes for a good rhythm in dialogue, so that there is a constant movement between characters.

Within that basic template you can and should vary the length. A garrulous character can be good fun in a comedy, especially if balanced with a monosyllabic one. Make sure there is some point to their talkativeness though.

Interruptions and pauses

In real life we interrupt each other all the time, and so should your characters. Indicate this with three dots at the end of the line, and start the next speech with three dots. Never use more than three dots (this is called an ellipsis). If you want to indicate a pause, for instance if the first speaker stops speaking because they've noticed something, and the second speaker cuts in before they can start again, then do so with the stage direction *pause*, not with extra dots.

We also interrupt ourselves, since thought moves faster than speech. This can be a normal part of a character's speech, or something they only do under stress.

Beginnings and endings

Most writers find that they fall into writing habits that they have to learn to watch out for, and one of the most common of these is starting every speech with 'Well'. You delete the 'well', and somehow the speech feels too abrupt, so you put it back in. Then you run your eye down the page and see a whole list of 'wells', possibly supported by a chorus of 'you knows' at the ends of speeches.

Take them all out. You will have to learn to do without them, however unnatural it feels. You will get used to writing without them, and then you will discover that in rehearsal the actors slip them back in – but not nearly as many as you had in the first place. It's best to keep quiet about it – the director will decide if they are necessary.

Once you have broken that habit you can do a lot with the beginnings and endings of speeches, which is where you have most of the audience's attention (we seem to be programmed that way).

An egotistical character will probably start every speech with 'I', a bossy one with 'you', a diffident one with 'er...' and so on. The last word of a speech is the most important one, however, and sometimes it is a question of re-arranging your grammar slightly to get the important word at the end. This matters a great deal in comedy, where you always want to create your main laugh at the end of a speech.

Case study: making the last word count

In our farce *Over Exposure*, we gave our protagonist this speech (he's thinking on his feet under pressure which explains the hesitations):

FRED: Oh good. Well, we take the photos, to, er, encourage her, to, um, express herself. Yes, that's it.

In rehearsal, the actor suggested that the following might get a laugh, since he was talking about a big-bosomed young woman:

FRED: Oh good. Well, we take the photos, to, er, encourage her, to, um, express herself. That way she makes a clean breast of it.

He was right to spot the possibility for a non-politically correct joke, and his version is quite funny, but it only took us a moment to realize that we needed the laugh to come on the last word of the speech:

FRED: Oh good. Well, we take the photos, to, er, encourage her, to, um, express herself. Yes, that's it. That way, she gets it all off her chest.

Even if you are not writing for laughs, this is a good basic rule to follow.

Group scenes

Once you have more than two characters on stage you will find that the dialogue becomes much more complicated and you will need to think about each character, particularly what is going through their mind when they are not speaking. It's not generally a good idea to have a character on stage and silent for long stretches of time, so don't let this happen unless you have a good reason for it. If you choose to do it, be absolutely sure why the character is silent, and think about how the actor is going to handle it.

There is a convention that actors should only have business (i.e. actions) while they are speaking. This is because the audience will automatically turn their attention to the character who is doing something rather than the one who is speaking. So if you have a silent character, they will have to be still as well. Of course rules are there to be broken. Alan Aykbourn brilliantly turned this convention on its head in his play *Absurd Person Singular* where throughout the whole of Act II, Eve is silently trying to commit suicide while the other characters talk – the brilliance is that the other characters, without realizing what she is trying to do, manage to thwart each attempt.

Exercise 12

Look at the list of settings you made for Exercises 1 and 2 and choose a setting for your two characters. Write a short dialogue between them.

Work in progress

Beryl has a precise way of speaking in line with her efficiency – she doesn't waste time and she doesn't waste words. She is grammatically correct.

Mel will generally use current slang, although speech patterns will vary depending on who she is talking to. She is not bothered about grammar.

Here is a monologue from Exercise 11 for each of our characters:

BERYL: I don't like being late, I do pride myself on being punctual, so when that receptionist had the temerity to say the doctor was seeing another patient because I had missed my slot, I made my feelings quite plain. I said 'I'm sorry I'm late, but I had to work overtime. My boss had an important piece of work which had to be done and I was the only one who could do it. It would have helped of course if my colleague, who knows about computers, had been prepared to stay and give me a hand, but apparently she had better things to do. Of course if you had given me a later appointment as requested then I would have been on time.' I could see that had put her in her place, in fact she looked quite drawn. So I said 'Still I suppose you have a problem fitting everyone in. The doctor will see me now will he?' And I left it at that.

MEL: Christmas dinner, what a fuss. I mean, no one sits down to a big family dinner these days, right? Look at Mum, she works herself into a right state and she still manages to burn the Brussels sprouts. So anyway I'm late, as usual, been up the pub with the girls, couple of Tequila Sunrises to get me in the festive spirit, you know how it is. So I come home and I'm stood on the doorstep and she throws a wobbly. So I says to her, I says 'Mum you're the best and you deserve a better daughter than me'. Well she only goes and agrees with me. Still we had a hug and a good laugh and I takes the dinner out of the oven, scrapes the sprouts into the bin and goes to watch telly with a tray on me knees. She's lovely my Mum.

We need a setting for Beryl and Mel. They could meet outside the Post Office or in the café, but the office is the most closed setting, and we already know that they work together. Here is a short dialogue for them:

BERYL: I can't stay on, I've got a doctor's appointment. You'll have to finish this.

MEL: Oh let's leave it till the morning, Beryl. We've only got to print off the spreadsheet.

BERYL: No, Mr Hubert wants those figures first thing and we don't all have your computer expertise.

MEL: Stay cool B. I'll come in early and knock it out before old Hubert even gets here.

BERYL: You, early? No, we'll do it now, come on.

Summary

In this chapter you have learnt:

- to give your characters distinctive speech patterns
- to make speech naturalistic without slavishly copying real speech
- to keep speeches short
- to understand why the last word in a speech is the most important.

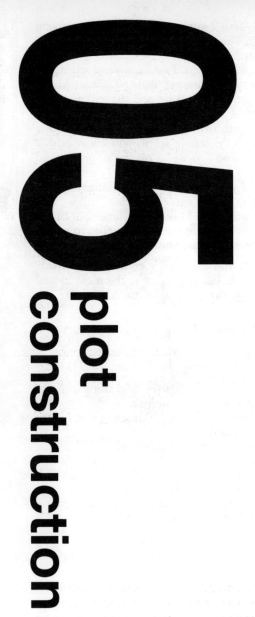

05

plot construction

In this chapter you will learn:
- more about conflict
- how to construct a plot
- about useful techniques.

The most common mistake that new playwrights make is: coming into a scene too early, and leaving it too late. Resist the urge to explain absolutely everything – it's good for us, the audience, to have to work something out for ourselves, to make the links, and to have to fill in the gaps.

Mark Smalley, BBC Radio 4 drama producer

'The structure of a play is always the story of how the birds came home to roost.' (Arthur Miller, playwright). On this simple premise hang all the great dramas: from tragedy to restoration comedy; from thriller to low farce. At the end of the day, a play is another way of telling a story and it is the way we construct that story that holds the audience's attention and sends them home satisfied.

All stories have a beginning, a middle and an end – but not necessarily in that order. And while most plays tend to work from a beginning through to an end in a constant timeline, there is nothing to stop the writer moving backwards and forwards in time and space, provided they follow the basic rules of construction, and take their audience with them.

Some writers have an in-born talent for construction without having to think about it. Others acquire it by watching or performing in plays and absorbing how other writers have achieved it. If you don't fall into any of these categories then it is worthwhile taking time to look at how a play works. Even if your preferred way of working is to take a couple of characters, put them in a situation and then see what happens, eventually, for the play to be coherent, you will need to check the construction.

How much notice should a writer take of the rules of construction? We all know that rules are made to be broken, but to break them you need to know them. Undeniably, certain types of construction have stood the test of time and certainly provide a good basis on which to create your play.

Conflict in plot

What is the driving force in all plays? The answer is conflict. A play, like life, has its ups and downs and, to take an analogy from music, these need to be orchestrated. While we might try to avoid conflict in our real life, it is the essential life force of drama. Without conflict nothing of interest happens.

Protagonists can be in conflict with other people, animals, inanimate objects, natural forces, social forces and themselves. This holds true for comedy as well as straight drama – they are just two sides of the same coin. The difference is the writer allows the audience to laugh at the conflict in a comedy.

However, don't confuse conflict with having a row with someone. While a good old slanging match between characters could be an integral and exciting part of the plot – and may even be the trigger for the drama to come – dramatic conflict works on a more subliminal level and is part of the subtext.

Exercise 13

Decide what the conflict between your two characters is when they are in the setting you have chosen. When you examine their characters, which you have chosen because they are strongly contrasted, you should find that they want different things out of the situation you have placed them in.

Simple construction

The simplest plot construction is made up of three parts.

- **Set-up.** Initially the protagonist is, if not at peace with the world, at least getting on with life. At this point he or she already has a history – often called the 'back-story' – a set of relationships and above all an immediate desire. It is this desire that is going to drive the plot forwards, and so it is the most important thing to show in the set-up.
- **Trigger.** Also known as the 'inciting incident', this means that something happens which puts the protagonist in a state of conflict. This is the most important moment in the play. It is the point of no return for the protagonist. The kaleidoscope has been shaken and the pieces won't settle until the resolution. Then they may settle back into their former pattern – but more likely they will form a completely different pattern.

  The trigger can be an external force over which the protagonist has no control or it can be a situation which has been activated by some flaw in their character. It may well arise out of something in the back-story. The plot will hang on the decisions the protagonist makes in response to the trigger.

- **Payoff.** Here we see the resolution of the conflict. It is more satisfying if the protagonist's own character traits enable them to win through – or perhaps causes them to lose. Otherwise it will be necessary to set up, earlier in the plot, the means of achieving resolution.

This construction holds true even if you are not following the conventional beginning, middle and end timeline.

Endings

Byron wrote: 'All tragedies end with a death and all comedies with a marriage'. That doesn't necessarily hold good today, but there should be a definite outcome to the protagonist's difficulties. Also, the outcome should appear to be the only one possible otherwise your audience will go home re-writing the end of your play. (See Chapter 06 for a full discussion of endings.)

Dramatic arc

The three-part construction is also called 'the dramatic arc', which is a visual way of describing how a simple play builds up and then curves down to the end. The arc is not symmetrical; it curves up gradually until it reaches the highest point and then curves down almost vertically. If you were to cut an egg in half longways it would look like a dramatic arc.

Exercise 14

Construct a simple plot for your two characters, in the setting you have chosen, consisting of a set-up, trigger and payoff. If you find that you need other characters to make the action happen, then go back to the list you created in Exercise 3. Before you add extra characters, repeat Exercises 5, 6, 7, 8 and 10 briefly for each one. Keep the plot very simple and short.

Compound construction

In a short one-act play the simple three-step construction is probably all that can be fitted in, but in a longer play the construction becomes more complicated.

Acts

Greek plays didn't have acts, but full-length plays from Ben Jonson onwards are generally divided into two or more. Modern plays tend to be in two acts, older plays in three, and we are used to five acts in Shakespeare plays, although the divisions were probably added at a later date. However, not all playwrights use them. Tennessee Williams' *A Streetcar Named Desire* has 11 scenes. Edward Bond's plays *Saved, Early Morning* and *The Pope's Wedding* have respectively 13, 21 and 16 scenes.

Acts operate as the skeleton on which the dramatic structure hangs. In the classic structure of a two- or three-act drama, the first act sets the premise for what is to come. A series of dramatic incidents are introduced, each one increasing the pressure on the protagonist, making the final resolution more difficult to attain. The arc now becomes a rising graph, with a series of peaks, each one higher than the previous one. Each section of the graph will follow the simple construction template of set-up, trigger and payoff. It contains the inciting moment and ends on a minor climax. The second act of a three-act play will expand on the subplots and obstacles. It should end with a crisis. After more twists, the final act culminates with the main climax and the resolution. Each act will have its own mini dramatic arc.

Act I needs to end on a high point that is strong enough to bring the audience back after the interval, but that is not a full-blown crisis. The whole act should build towards this moment. Act II needs to resume the conflict but at a slightly lower level, because the interval will have broken the audience's concentration. Give them a little time to get back into the play, and then start building towards the climax.

Scenes

Traditionally, each act is broken up into a series of scenes which are marked by changes of scenery, or the curtain opening or closing, or a change of lighting where neither of these is available. However, the definition of a scene is extremely loose and may not be marked in any obvious way, so that the audience is barely aware of the change. Scenes show a change in place and/or time, but can also mark an emotional change without any movement in place or time. They can move the plot backwards in time as well as forwards. They can also encompass two different stories going on at the same time, using all or part of the same set.

Even a play with continuous action could be said to have a series of scenes. Each time a character enters or exits the dynamics of the play change, and for all intents and purposes this starts a new scene. The same holds true when there are only two characters and no entrances and exits. The balance of power or the emotional balance will constantly change between them and each change creates a new scene.

Scenes should end in a way that leaves something open, a miniature trigger without a payoff. This will move the action on to the next scene and keep the audience in a state of anticipation. It can be a line of dialogue, an action, a visual image or a sound effect, but it is usually known as a curtain line. The best curtain lines arise out of some aspect of the conflict within the play.

Case study: recognizing a change of scene

At the start of our play *Ashes to Ashes* Margaret is in the ascendant, but as she and Dilys revert to childhood, Dilys is in the ascendant. The balance of power between them see-saws back and forth and each change marks a new scene even though the action of the play is continuous and on one set. In this section, Margaret is bullying Dilys at first, but suddenly Dilys turns on her. A new scene starts at that point.

MARGARET: This is serious, you great fat lump. You could go to prison for what you did.

DILYS: I didn't do nothing. It weren't my fault I couldn't find them pills. You said they was in the cabinet but they wasn't.

MARGARET: So you say, but supposing you didn't look properly. In fact how do I know you looked at all?

DILYS: Course I looked. I told you, I pulled everything out, they wasn't there.

MARGARET: Look, it's alright, I won't tell anyone, but we must stick to the same story.

New scene starts here

DILYS: Who says? I could say I went shopping. On my own. I could say you was here with him all the time. Nothing to do with me.

MARGARET: You wouldn't do that.

DILYS: I could.

MARGARET: But we're mates.

DILYS: So?

Construction step-by-step

The set-up is the situation that pertains just before the play opens.

> ### Case study: setting up the situation
>
> For *Whatever You Want* the set-up would be:
>
> Raymond is trying to get organized for Monday's business in the back-street beauty salon which he runs with his wife Margaret. He's paid for Margaret to have a weekend at a health farm, so he's behind with the chores that she normally nags him to do. He's being hampered by Dilys, an old friend of Margaret's who turned up at the weekend, after many years without contact, looking for somewhere to stay after the break-up of her marriage.

Beginnings

It may seem obvious that all plays have a beginning, but you are telling a story and where you start it is very important. We all know the person who starts to tell you a story, then stops and goes back a bit because they've missed out an important part, then repeats what they have already told you. You don't have that luxury in the theatre so picking the right moment is paramount if you want to grab the audience's attention straight away. Playwrights have one advantage over novelists here because while a reader might discard a book if the first few paragraphs don't attract them, someone who has paid for a seat and is stuck in the middle of a row is unlikely to walk out after the first few minutes. However, it is best not to try your audience's patience, so think carefully about what you want to achieve in these opening moments.

In the simple, three-part construction we saw the protagonist is at peace with the world until something happens to change things (the trigger). However, it can make for better drama if the play starts as close to the trigger as possible. The previous background to the situation, the protagonist's character and emotional state can then be fed to the audience through exposition (see below). This way the audience's attention is grabbed from the outset. Although is it a good idea to start as close to the trigger as possible, it is true that the further into the story you start, the more complicated the set-up will be and the more exposition might be needed.

Case study: beginnings

For *Whatever You Want* we needed Margaret to have been away for the weekend, so we decided that her husband had treated her to the relaxing weekend at a health farm. When she returns, she reveals that he misread the brochure and she ended up in a seminar for women on running a small business, and that she is now all fired-up and full of new ideas for their beauty salon – the last thing he wants. The weekend away is not just integrated into the plot, it is the trigger that sets the whole story off. (And her husband's flaw of laziness leads to the events that cause his problems).

Exposition

Exposition is the information the audience needs to understand the story of the play.

It includes:

- information from the set-up
- past histories of each of the characters (their back-stories).

It does not include information that arises during the course of the play. This type of information will happen quite naturally through dialogue, but exposition has to be fed to the audience in a controlled manner.

Inevitably the writer is tempted to get it out of the way early on, but this is usually a mistake. The audience will immediately twig if the writer tries to introduce large chunks of background information which are out of keeping with the rest of the dialogue. It is often better to feed information in small doses throughout the play. This not only keeps the audience intrigued, but also makes it easier to incorporate the exposition into the dialogue in a natural way.

While it is essential to ensure that the audience is in possession of all the facts necessary to understanding the story, getting the balance right is tricky. Give the audience too much explanation and they don't have to do any work. Give them too little and they will struggle to understand the plot and be annoyed with an ending which seems to come out of the blue. Even when you think you have got the balance right there will always be some in the audience who will get it and some who won't.

Occasionally writers produce plays with no exposition at all – Harold Pinter is a prime example. It creates an atmosphere of mystery and puzzlement, but also leaves the audience unsure about the characters, and in particular which character deserves their sympathy.

Top tip

In your first few drafts, you may well write pages and pages of exposition, but later you will need to remove most of this. Writing yourself in is fine, but don't forget to edit yourself out. Decide what is the absolute minimum the audience needs to know to understand the play and settle for that. In truth, it is probably still too much.

Obstacles

Once you have established the protagonist's desire, and the conflict which frustrates that desire, then the plot needs a series of obstacles that raise the stakes and increase the conflict. The inciting incident triggers the problem and the new and increasingly difficult obstacles intensify it. As soon as the protagonist overcomes one, another comes along and these should increase in intensity as the pressure builds. In other words, the obstacles are what drive the rising graph of the dramatic arc. Remember, it is more satisfying if each new obstacle springs from the protagonist's own character flaws or the decisions they have made to overcome the earlier obstacles. As the protagonist overcomes each new obstacle, there will be a minor climax, and each new obstacle should be more challenging than the previous one. Towards the end there is a crisis when it seems the protagonist is not going to overcome the obstacles, followed by the dramatic climax.

Twists

Another way of creating obstacles, and to keep the audience guessing, is to introduce a twist. This can be in the shape of a new character or a totally unexpected revelation. Whatever the twist, it should completely alter the direction of the play. There is a convention that a major twist should come between half and two thirds of the way into the plot, but the exact spot will be dictated by the type of plot and whether there will be more than one twist. There can be two or more in thrillers, whodunnits and comedies.

Reverses

These are similar to twists but completely reverse a situation. A character whom the audience believes is a hero is shown to be the villain or vice versa. This completely alters the audience's reliance on what has gone before. When writing a play with a reverse it is important to check that all the dialogue makes sense both ways.

Case study: reversing the plot

In Robert Thomas's *Trap for a Lonely Man* the protagonist has reported his wife missing and yet a woman is claiming to be her. We empathize with his nightmare because no one, not even the police, believes his claim that she is an impostor. Right at the end the situation is reversed when he confesses to his wife's murder and the audience learns the bogus wife is a set-up by the police to trap him.

Crisis

This is the point towards the end of the play when it looks as if the protagonist is doomed to failure. In line with the saying 'it is always darkest just before the dawn', the protagonist should have the most pressure put on them just before the play reaches its final climax. The crisis must be bigger than all the previous obstacles and should look insurmountable. The type of crisis you devise, and whether the protagonist does or doesn't overcome it, will depend on the nature of the play. A thriller will need a moment of pure terror, which probably means a physical threat, whereas a psychological study will need an emotional crisis, perhaps a moment of revelation or a secret exposed.

Case study: escalating crises

In *Long Day's Journey into Night* by Eugene O'Neill the protagonist Edmund faces a rising series of crises, first as he confronts his mother's addiction, then his father's tyranny and in the final scene the worst one of all, his older brother's confession that he always hated Edmund. His brother's love had been the one constant in Edmund's life and the confession completes his realization that there is to be no happy ending for him.

Exercise 15

Expand your simple plot to create a crisis for the protagonist(s).

Turning point and obligatory moment

The turning point in a drama is when the protagonist has to face up to the pressures being placed upon them. As a result of confronting their difficulties, characters grow and develop. The reward for this journey can be to achieve their goal, but equally it can lead to the realization that the goal was never that important.

In tragedy, there is a convention known as the obligatory moment, when the protagonist achieves insight into their behaviour and accepts responsibility for their actions. It is not strictly speaking obligatory but most plots, even those that are not tragedies, function more effectively with one.

Climax

The highest point of the dramatic arc is the climax. This is the moment that the whole play is centred on – where all the plotting has been leading. The protagonist faces their biggest challenge and either wins or loses depending on the play. Life will never be the same again.

The climax comes directly before the resolution and its placing is crucially important. If it is placed too early the audience could well expect something else to happen, an even bigger climax perhaps, and if it is too near the end the play will finish in a rush.

The incidents that lead up to the climax should occur at accelerating speed, but the climax itself must be taken more slowly. The whole play has been heading for this moment – indeed probably the entire lives of the characters, from way back in their back-stories, have been building towards this climax, so don't rush it. (For two detailed case studies of pacing a climax see Chapter 08.)

Resolution

By this stage the audience should have been taken on a rollercoaster ride, but now everything is gradually slowing down. All they want is for everything to be neatly tied up, all the explanations given – what they don't want is for it to go on too long.

The resolution:

- ties up loose ends
- brings the play to its close
- provides a comment on the ending.

It is important in that it is the last contact the audience has with the work, and therefore it sets the emotional tone for what they take away with them.

Exercise 16

From the crisis, work out the stages that will move your plot to its climax and resolution. You may find that your original payoff has to be altered. Do not at this stage allow your plot to develop into a full-length play – aim for a short but well-crafted scene.

Subplots

Subplots develop naturally out of the back-stories of the minor characters, and out of their involvement with the protagonist. A subplot can reinforce the play's message, or emphasize the protagonist's achievement.

Each subplot needs:

- an inciting incident
- a climax
- a resolution.

For instance, if the protagonist wins through a series of difficulties, a subplot could show another character failing to conquer a similar set of problems. If the protagonist is doomed to failure through some character flaw, then the subplot could show a minor character who risked less but was more successful.

Case study: the importance of a subplot

In *A Man for All Seasons*, Robert Bolt told the story of Thomas More and Henry VIII going head to head over Henry's divorce. The subplot was about More's family, whose fate of course was bound up with his, so that every decision he made had ramifications for them. The subplot greatly enlarged the scope of the play, and increased the human interest angle.

Plot techniques

Rule of three

A well-known rule for political speech writers is 'tell them what you are about to tell them, then tell them what you want to tell them, then tell them what you've just told them.' In other words, say something three times and it will sink in. In a play you should use the same rule for important information. Tell your audience three times – but do it subtly and in three different ways and through different characters. Only use this rule for truly important information.

Show don't tell

Plays are a visual medium and actions speak louder than words. The audience will expect to see what is happening rather than being told about it. If you want to set up a character's short temper, try to avoid having them say 'I've got a short temper', or having another character say 'he's got a short temper'. Far better to introduce a small event that will cause the character to fly off the handle.

Of course sometimes you might need a character to make statements about themselves in order to reveal their true nature. A bully might say 'now don't you cross me, I've got a short temper'; a deluded character might say 'I never lose my temper'. Subsequent events would need to confirm or deny the truth of these statements.

The uninformed character and the informed audience

New writers are often tempted by the simple trick of having a character who knows as little about the set-up as the audience. If your play is set in an office for instance, a new member of staff on their first day can be introduced. Other characters have to explain the set-up to them. Someone tells the new person the history, the audience is clued in, the play can proceed. This can work well if the new member of staff is essential to the plot. Otherwise you now have an extra character, who may have no other function, your audience may have fallen asleep while listening to the explanation and you've broken one of the cardinal rules (show don't tell).

It only works if there is a point in the back-story where it is perfectly natural for one character to be in ignorance. If you start your play at this moment, then the information given to that character is also given to the audience as exposition.

Although it can keep an audience interested if the drama throws up unexpected twists, turns and shocks, there are occasions when the audience needs to know something that one or more of the characters don't know. For a case study see Chapter 11.

Another way of keeping the audience's interest is to feed them some information, but to hold back a crucial piece until later.

 Case study: delaying exposition to the audience

In *Whatever You Want* only the audience knows that Ray has been to see a solicitor in an attempt to sabotage Margaret's efforts. When he returns, he clearly thinks he has won, but we chose to delay the revelation of how exactly, by having Dilys interrupt at the crucial moment.

Foreshadowing and reincorporation

As well as feeding information from the past, the writer will also have to incorporate into the dialogue what is to come – this is called foreshadowing.

To ensure that the ending doesn't come as a bolt from the blue, you will need to foreshadow it in subtle ways. The audience should not be aware that the information you are giving them is going to affect the end, but when you have achieved a satisfying resolution, they will look back and work things out. This is particularly important with character traits and flaws. Foreshadowing can also be used with incidents from the character's past, which can suddenly become important in the resolution of the play.

Reincorporation is similar to foreshadowing but it relates more to props and business. It is a favourite of television sitcom writers but it is a useful and satisfying tool for all writers. It simply means that very early on an apparently innocuous prop or characteristic is established, which later turns out to be the hinge of the whole plot, or the solution to the problem that the play explores. In between, the item is not mentioned, so that its reappearance comes as a surprise.

Hooks

These are similar to foreshadowing and are introduced throughout the play to allow the writer to hang a little piece of plot on.

Some writers put hooks in as they write in case they come in useful later on. They can then go back and take out the ones which weren't needed. Or they can leave them in as red herrings to keep the audience guessing. If they are not there and you find you need them, go back and put them in.

Case study: hooks

In *Over Exposure* we initially made Hans an illegal immigrant to ensure there was a reason why he was frightened of the police, and to give him a hazy grasp of English. Eventually we dropped the illegal immigrant hook because another plot line made him nervous of the police.

Reported action

Shakespeare wrote some of his most beautiful lines when describing something that had happened off stage – a battle for instance. However, conventions change and now, thanks to television and film, we are used to seeing everything before our very eyes. We don't, as a result, have much patience with reported action. Use it, by all means, but only if it moves the play forward and reveals something about your characters. Is the one doing the reporting a liar? Are the listening characters gullible enough to fall for it?

Top tip

Take a simple story such as Robin Hood, Samson and Delilah, Adam and Eve or The Ugly Duckling. Identify the set-up, the trigger, the conflict, the unexpected development, the subplot and the payoff.

Work in progress

The conflict is that both women need to get away on time but Beryl can only manage it if she persuades Mel to stay and help her. Beryl is conscientious and wants to leave things ready for the morning: Mel just wants to get away. Here is a simple plot with a set-up, trigger and payoff:

Set-up

Beryl is tidying her desk ready to leave the office. Mel is sitting at a computer terminal. The clock on the wall shows 16:55.

BERYL: *(putting on her coat)* I'm leaving now Melanie.

MEL: Okey dokey. Have a good time.

BERYL: Actually I have to get to the doctor's, they wouldn't give me a later appointment.

MEL: You aren't ill or nothing?

Trigger

Phone rings and Beryl answers it.

Conflict

BERYL: Yes Mr Hubert ... oh, well, I haven't ... yes of course right away.

She puts down the phone and takes off her coat.

MEL: What did he want?

BERYL: His meeting's been moved forward. He wants those figures by nine tomorrow.

MEL: Do it first thing, it'll be OK.

BERYL: No, we need to finish it now. Just show me what I have to do.

MEL: Just click on that.

Beryl leans over Mel takes the mouse and clicks. Printer starts printing sheets of paper.

BERYL: Is that all?

MEL: I told you it was easy.

Payoff

Mel picks up the printed sheets and gives them to Beryl who exits.

By adding a crisis to the simple plot we can expand the scene, and resolution of the crisis brings in another character. As a result, the payoff changes. We pick up the scene at Mel's penultimate speech:

MEL: Just click on that. *(She stares at the computer screen.)* Oh for crying out loud.

Crisis

BERYL: What, what's happened?

MEL: It's crashed. It's no good Beryl, we might as well go home.

BERYL: Can't you do something?

MEL: No. *(Sudden thought.)* Yes I can. *(She dials a number, speaks into the phone.)* Stevie? Hi, it's Mel, ummm I got a problem ... *(giggles)* no not like that ... me computer's crashed ... can you come and look at ... like now. Ciao, Stevie. *(She replaces the phone and turns to Beryl.)* Steve's coming up to have a look.

BERYL: But he's not IT support. I'll phone them, they can't all have gone home.

MEL: They'll take forever, you know what they're like. Steve's a fast worker.

BERYL: He does know about computers?

MEL: Well he's good with his hands *(beat)* so they tell me anyway.

Steve enters and looks at Mel's screen.

STEVE: What have you done to it? Shift yourself then.

Mel gets up and Steve sits in her place and starts typing. Mel hangs over his shoulder.

BERYL: Will this take long?

MEL: *(to Steve)* It's alright, there's no rush.

BERYL: We have some urgent figures to finish and I have to get away.

STEVE: *(to Mel)* No wonder it crashed, how many games have you downloaded?

Steve continues typing.

STEVE: Is that what you were working on?

He gets up and Mel sits down.

MEL: There you are Beryl, panic over. Thanks Steve, you're a honey.

STEVE: I aim to please.

BERYL: Could we just get this finished please?

MEL: Like I said, just click on that.

Beryl leans over Mel, takes the mouse and clicks. Printer starts printing sheets of paper.

BERYL: Is that all?

MEL: I told you it was easy.

BERYL: *(awkward pause)* Thanks Mel, I'll, er, I'll make it up to you. And you Steve.

Mel picks up the printed sheets and gives them to Beryl who exits smiling.

Payoff

MEL: *(to Steve)* You off home or do you fancy a drink?

Summary

In this chapter you have learnt:

- how to construct a simple plot
- how to add complications to a plot
- how to handle expositions, crises and climaxes.

06

endings

In this chapter you will learn:
- about types of ending
- what is needed for a satisfying ending
- how to construct an ending.

The most common mistake that new playwrights make is: to assume that we're looking for more of the same. Every production is a journey of discovery, and the joy of that discovery accounts for some of the excitement in the finished work.

Jessica Dromgoule, radio drama producer

Endings are important, but a lot of writers don't seem to realize this. By the time they come to write the ending they are tired, they have had their fun with the plot and the characters, and so the ending can seem hurried and unsatisfying. And yet the ending is what the audience takes home with them. It is the vehicle by which they absorb your play's message, or rate its entertainment value.

In life there are very few endings. The story always goes on, rather like a soap opera. In novels, films and plays there have to be endings, and for this reason endings present the greatest challenge to a writer.

The main function of the ending is to send the audience away satisfied. This doesn't mean that there has to be a happy ending, or even an ending that ties up loose ends. It only means that the expectations of the audience have to have been fulfilled. In a well-written play the ending seems inevitable once we get there, and yet unpredictable on the journey to reach it. The best endings are both surprising and expected. This is because the writer has set little clues throughout the play that make perfect sense once you reach the end but which are too small to be noticed at the time.

Top tip

Some writers like to draft the ending before they write anything else, or at the very least work out how the plot will end. Murder mysteries are probably better written this way because the writer really needs to know whodunnit before they start. Others like to start writing and see what happens. Whichever you choose, be sure to allocate plenty of time for writing and re-writing the last six to ten pages of the script.

Types of endings

There are two types of ending.

- **Closed.** A closed ending is the most conventional, in which all plot strands are resolved and the audience is given the answer to every question.
- **Open.** An open ending will still resolve most plot strands, but will leave the audience to work out for themselves one or two of the questions. A completely open ending, with nothing resolved, is almost impossible to achieve successfully. Basically, a completely open ending means that you avoid the third aspect of basic plot construction, the payoff, which in turn means that there is no resolution and no catharsis for the audience.

If the writer feels absolutely compelled to convey something to the audience and only an open ending will do it, then that passion will underlie the play and make the ending inevitable. If the writer has simply run out of ideas and thinks an open ending is a clever way to solve their problem, then the audience will see straight through it.

A conventional plot structure will take the protagonist through one or more crises to a climax, and the ending will be shortly after the climax. It works particularly well if you can devise a turning point for the protagonist within the climax and move quickly to the ending from there.

Case study: open endings

Samuel Becket was a master of the open ending and now that his plays are so well-established audiences accept them. In *Waiting for Godot* for instance, by the end, Godot hasn't turned up, nothing has changed since the play opened and Vladimir and Estragon are still convinced that Godot will come tomorrow. Becket was saying something about the human condition and that is the key to the successful open ending.

Emotional content

An ending can be:

- happy
- sad
- a mixture.

In a romantic story, for instance, a happy ending brings the lovers together, all problems resolved (*Cinderella*). A sad ending keeps the lovers apart (*Romeo and Juliet*). However, a mixed ending can be happy/sad or sad/happy. Happy/sad might end with a wedding, but includes a little incident that shows the marriage will have problems. Sad/happy might keep the protagonist away from their desired lover, but show them meeting someone else just before the curtain comes down.

Whatever you do, don't force a happy ending onto a play just because you think it will make the play more saleable. This has been known to happen in film versions of plays and novels and it very rarely works. Remember, the ending has to seem inevitable, so a happy ending must grow out of what has gone before.

Even good writers can trip up over an ending.

Case study: problem endings

When George Bernard Shaw wrote *Pygmalion*, it seemed entirely logical to him that Eliza Doolittle would not marry Professor Higgins at the end. She was too intelligent, he felt, to marry someone who had treated her so badly, and Higgins was a confirmed bachelor anyway. Unfortunately audiences felt differently, and Shaw became so exasperated that he wrote an essay explaining this for published editions of the play script. He refused to change the ending in the stage version, but when it came to making a film of *Pygmalion* he had to accept an ending that implied a marriage between Eliza and Higgins.

While Shaw might have been right that, in real life, Eliza would not have fallen in love with the short-tempered and selfish Higgins, he had unfortunately written a play that conformed to a well-established convention of romantic comedy – one that goes back to at least *The Taming of the Shrew*. In this convention a couple who start at loggerheads end up in love, and Shaw was not quite clever enough to write a play that could challenge the convention.

Exercise 17

However your plot currently ends, devise endings that fit the other two categories. Decide which is most suitable.

Further considerations

Deus Ex Machina

Literally this means 'a god out of the machine' and refers to the habit, in Greek drama, of resolving a plot by the sudden intervention of one of the gods. The Greeks did believe that humans were the playthings of the gods, and subject to their every whim, and so this type of ending was culturally acceptable.

Today it is often referred to as 'bringing on the cavalry', in other words a surprise rescue out of the blue. This type of ending is most likely to leave an audience feeling cheated, except possibly as a humorous way of ending a comedy. It's best avoided though.

> **Top tip**
> If you feel tempted to resolve your plot in this way, it's a sign that the plot needs further work.

Surprise endings

As explained above, this does not mean suddenly resolving matters with an intervention from outside the play's own internal logic. It means that, just when it looks as if everything is resolved, it turns out there is one last shocking throw of the dice to come.

A variation of this type of ending is often used in television and film thrillers, where a character appears to be trapped and doomed but is saved by another character turning up at the last minute. This is harder to do on stage, but the key is to convince the audience that the second character is completely unable to help, and to allow enough on-stage time to pass for that character to be half forgotten, so that when they do appear at the last minute it is both a shock and a relief.

> **Case study: surprise endings**
> A good example is *Wait Until Dark*, in which an intruder attempts to murder a blind woman in her own flat. After many twists and turns it looks as if she has killed him, but as she sags with relief he rears up and attacks her once more, despite being mortally wounded.

Conflict resolution

The ending will need to show the resolution of the main conflicts in the play, but will not necessarily resolve all the levels of conflict. This is where understanding your theme is important, because the most important conflict will be the one most closely related to the theme. For more on themes see Chapter 07.

The protagonist and other characters

The ending is always about the protagonist – it finishes their story in some way. Even if you choose a very open ending, in which the protagonist appears to just carry on with life, they are still the most important character, so start by deciding how their story will end. Remember that the audience will have built up a relationship with the protagonist and the emotional atmosphere of the play will have caused them to have expectations about the ending. You can choose not to fulfil these expectations, but do it deliberately, not accidentally.

The stories of the other characters will need resolving as well, but they mustn't be allowed to distract from the ending of the protagonist's story. If you are using a narrator, then they can give the audience a brief overview of what happened to each character after the story of the play ended.

Exercise 18

Examine your plot and make sure that the resolution is fully focused on the protagonist(s) and not minor characters.

Pace

Don't rush towards the ending, let it unfold. In particular, look at the potential for emotional swings. If you are heading for a happy ending, have a moment of doubt just before it is achieved. With an unhappy ending, have a moment of false hope. You are playing with the audience's emotional responses but this is the one time you can get away with it. They will sense the ending coming and should be following every change with bated breath.

Catharsis

This Greek word describes the effect on the audience of most endings – after the build-up of tension and emotion throughout the play, the resolution at the end provides release and relief. It is most clearly seen in thrillers and mysteries, but most plays have a degree of catharsis in the ending. Don't underestimate the importance of this – part of the function of drama is to take people out of themselves for a while, and then send them back to their everyday lives feeling refreshed and emotionally renewed. Catharsis achieves this goal.

There are writers who deliberately avoid catharsis. They want their audience to leave feeling unsettled, usually because they want their play to be thought-provoking in some way. Their audience will be small, but enthusiastic.

How to construct an ending

When you are in the process of writing a play there is nothing inevitable about the ending at all. Some writers do start with a clear idea of where they are going, but not all. A play that starts with a strong plot idea will probably include a sense of what the ending will be, but if you start with the characters and build the plot around them as you write then you may have no idea where you are heading. Even if you start off quite sure about your ending, you may find that when you get there it doesn't work, and you have to look at alternatives.

Look back at the earliest decisions you made about the play. What is it about, at the deepest level? What is its world view? Is it, for instance, about little people being crushed by the system? This would give a sad ending, such as in *Death of a Salesman* where Willie Loman kills himself to prove a point. If the system is defeated, the ending could be simplistically happy or, more realistically, a mixture of the two, such as in *The Winslow Boy* by Terence Rattigan. In this play the people who take on the system and fight for the honour of the falsely accused boy all pay a price for their involvement.

Case study: devising an ending

When we started writing *Whatever You Want* we thought we knew roughly how it would end, because we wanted to write a farce with a woman as the central character. We thought that Margaret would get herself into deeper and deeper trouble, trying to get what she wanted, but it didn't work out that way.

For a start her character turned out to be too direct – the protagonist in a farce has to be devious. Also, she had one redeeming characteristic – she did care about her friend Dilys, and in a turning-point scene she stops doing what she wants to do and spends time helping Dilys. We needed a different ending, and we decided that each of the four characters would get what they wanted, but not in the way that they expected.

So Margaret, who wants to run her own business, ends up as Dilys's personal manager instead of a beauty salon owner. Dilys, who wants to indulge her obsessions with food and romance ends up writing slushy bestsellers instead of getting back with husband Steve. And the two husbands, Steve and Ray, who just want a quiet life, end up sharing a bungalow by the sea. Ray loses Margaret but gains Steve, and Margaret loses her business but gains the lifestyle. Dilys loses her marriage but gains endless romantic dreaming and eating in the best restaurants. Steve loses Dilys but is able to take up the offer of early retirement.

Exercise 19

Before reading the next chapter, write out your scene in full. For the purposes of this exercise it only needs to be one or two pages long.

Work in progress

At the end of Chapter 05 the ending for our play did not focus on the main protagonist, Beryl, so it clearly needs changing. A happy ending would see Beryl getting the figures out and getting to the doctor's on time – maybe Mel would do the figures and Steve would give her a lift. A sad ending would see both of these goals frustrated, perhaps with the computer crashing again, and a mixed ending would let her achieve one goal but not the other.

We pick up the scene just before the end:

BERYL: Could we just get this finished please?

The phone rings on Beryl's desk, she answers it.

BERYL: Yes Mr Hubert, I have them right here.
MEL: *(to Steve)* You off home then or do you fancy a drink?
STEVE: Could do.

They start to move off the stage.

BERYL: You can't go yet. How do I print them off?

Mel comes back.

MEL: *(irritably)* For goodness sake, just click on that.

Mel and Steve exit. Beryl clicks, the printer makes a strange noise, smoke pours out of it. Phone starts ringing.

BERYL: *(calling)* Mel, Steve, come back!

This is an open ending but clearly not a happy one. The scene has come to a natural conclusion, but there is no final resolution, in fact the printer going wrong could be seen as another obstacle to be overcome. Beryl's behaviour once again has irritated Mel, particularly because she is more interested in Steve.

Summary

In this chapter you have learnt:

- about the importance of endings
- how to make the ending seem inevitable
- how to devise an ending.

07

deeper issues

The main thing I look for in a new script is: something that goes beyond formula and stereotypes, something with living and breathing characters and heart.

Abigail Davies, script editor and producer

Deeper issues are all aspects of a play that are important, and in some cases essential, but that are not immediately obvious.

Over the years there has been much debate about how many basic plots there are. Suggested answers range from just one – the quest – to long lists of different essential plots. There is no one definitive list. Similar debates rage around themes and messages – what they are, how many there are and so on. Rather than add to these debates, we are going to try to clarify what you need to know as a writer in a practical way about these deeper issues.

Deep structure

Plots

We all recognize certain basic stories when we come across them, such as:

- boy meets girl, boy loses girl, boy finds girl
- mysterious stranger rides into town and solves the problem
- young person goes through traumas to reach adulthood.

It is perfectly acceptable to work within these templates, in fact, however original you try to be, you will probably find one of the world's great stories is hiding inside your plot. However, because they are so clichéd, these stories are both a blessing and a curse for the writer. The blessing is that the audience will find it easy to follow the story and to understand its underlying logic. The curse is that you may end up writing something predictable and boring. The answer is to be aware of what you are doing, and to look for a fresh and relevant approach.

Stereotype and archetype

Stereotype and archetype are terms in constant use but what do they mean? Strictly speaking the word archetype means an original or prototype, and stereotype means a shared set of values or characteristics.

In drama, however, an archetype not only means the original, but also all subsequent versions of the original. It is universal and occurs across history and in different cultures. A good example of an archetypal story is The Quest. It recurs throughout storytelling history and across all cultures. It comes up fresh every time because it allows for new permutations that are relevant to the particular audience it is aimed at, and flexibly adapts to new cultures.

Archetypal quest stories include:

- Jason on his quest for the Golden Fleece
- the Hindu Rama searching for his wife Sita
- the Chinese Monkey-King sent west by Buddha to find holy scriptures
- Indiana Jones searching for the Holy Grail.

A stereotype on the other hand defines people in categories, allocating characteristics based on membership of a certain group, rather than their individual characters. Stereotypes in drama allow an audience to quickly connect with a character, but they make for a predictable and uninteresting play if over-used.

Note that in feedback and critical appraisals the term stereotype is often loosely used in a negative way, implying that the writer has mindlessly copied an existing plot or character without adding anything new.

Parallelism

Both plot and characters need to have twin aspects, each feeding a different storytelling need:

- the need to know what happens next
- the emotional exploration.

The suspense plot – or the need to know what happens next – is the aspect of the play that keeps the audience in their seats. So your plot will need an element of suspense, a question that is asked at the beginning and that the audience wants answered. The protagonist will need a characteristic that drives them through this element of the plot. It can be extremely simple or hideously complicated.

Having kept the audience's attention with the suspense plot, the writer can then feed their deeper need for emotional exploration. This aspect of both plot and character answers the questions:

- why does the protagonist act the way they do?
- why do they make those particular choices?
- why does that particular crisis arise?

The answers will lie in the psychology of each of the characters and the chemistry that arises between them.

Case study: parallelism

In *Whose Life Is It Anyway* by Brian Clark, the suspense element of the plot asks the simple question 'Will the protagonist live or die?'. The protagonist has the characteristic of determination to pursue his desire to die and the emotional part of the plot follows his journey.

In a traditional farce, on the other hand, the suspense plot will be exceptionally complicated, and the protagonist's characteristic can be quite simple, so that in our farce *Over Exposure* Fred's simple desire to become Mayor drives him through the twists and turns of the plot.

Exercise 20

Examine your scene and differentiate between the emotional plot and the suspense plot. If one is missing, you need to rethink.

Underlying themes

These are really about you as a writer and what motivates you. When you look at any writer's body of work you will see recurrent themes appearing throughout. Shakespeare was fascinated by kingship and the transmission of power, whereas Tom Stoppard keeps returning to the question of the nature of morality. The good news is you won't have to work at discovering your themes, they will emerge naturally as you write. You will, however, have to put some effort into understanding your interest in them, and exploring different aspects of that interest.

So, themes are the big issues that underlie any story. There is a wide range of themes reflecting all levels of human experience, and some have a more enduring fascination than others. On the whole we are more interested in love-themed stories than in relationship-breakdown stories, and more interested in war stories than poverty stories. If you choose an unusual theme, increase its appeal by including aspects of a more popular theme. For instance, Tom Stoppard's play *Hapgood* is based around quantum physics, a difficult topic for most people, but includes elements of the more accessible romantic comedy genre.

A theme, therefore, while underpinning your play, doesn't dictate the shape of the plot or the ending. But it does give a deep coherence without which a play can feel thin and unsatisfying.

Case study: theme

The underlying theme of *Whatever You Want* is frustration – like most comedies it starts with a negative. When we wrote the darker version about Margaret and Dilys, *Ashes to Ashes*, we used the same theme but explored it in different ways. In this version Margaret has married Max instead of Ray, and his intransigent slobbishness and insensitivity has cranked her frustration up to such a level that it has driven her mad.

Top tip

Once you've roughed out your play, stop and consider the underlying theme or themes. When you have identified what these are, it is worth going through the script and cutting anything that isn't relevant to the theme, and altering scenes to better reflect the theme.

Subplots

Subplots don't have to have the same theme as the main plot, but there is a satisfying completeness if subplots are thematically linked to the main plot.

Case study: theme in subplots

In an episode of the American sitcom *Frasier*, the main plot was based on Frasier's unhappiness that his father's live-in physiotherapist Daphne was having her boyfriend to stay overnight. Finally he could take it no more and Daphne agreed to find alternative accommodation. After one weekend without her, Frasier and his father, Martin, were at each other's throats. So Daphne told Frasier a totally implausible story that her boyfriend was impotent. As long as Frasier could believe that the couple were not having sex he was happy.

The first subplot concerned Frasier's brother Niles who was devastated that he had not been invited to a society party, but was soothed when the host explained that his invitation had been eaten by the host's dog. The second subplot concerned Martin who, despite constantly over-indulging, blamed his tight trousers on the laundry.

The theme for all three plot strands was self-delusion, and in all three storylines the characters maintained their delusions through to the end.

Messages

Like theme, the message of your play will also be affected by your own world view.

Are you:

• an optimist or a pessimist?
• left wing or right wing?
• religious or atheistic?

Some writers are more message-driven than others, and are determined to make their point through their plays. However, they have to beware of the pitfall of being too heavy handed, which is off-putting for an audience.

Case study: messages

Brecht's *Mother Courage*, set during the Thirty Year's War (a seventeenth century conflagration which involved most of Europe), was written at the start of the Second World War to draw people's attention to the rise of Nazi Germany. By focusing on one person and her family, Brecht made it easier for the audience to identify with the message that war means profits for some people.

Even those writers, like us, who are not focused on a message, will find one coming through. The message of *Whatever You Want* is 'what you think you want may not be the answer to your problems, and you can find the answers in unexpected ways'. All four characters know what they want and think they know how to achieve it, and yet the final solution turns out to be quite different from what they expected. In the companion piece *Ashes to Ashes* the message changed: not getting what you want leads to moral breakdown and ultimate insanity. It only features the Dilys and Margaret characters, and Margaret's frustration has led her to murder her husband.

Emotional charge and emotional journey

If you look at theme and message together, you will find a play's emotional charge.

This can be:

- positive
- negative
- a mixture of the two.

If your theme is war, and your message is 'war is pointless' then the emotional charge is negative. If your message is 'war produces heroism' then the emotional charge is positive, and if your message is 'war is terrible but is necessary to combat evil' then you have a positive/negative (or ironic) emotional charge.

For your ending to have that feeling of inevitability, it should reflect the underlying emotional charge of the play.

Case study: emotional charge

The emotional charge of *Whatever You Want* is positive, in *Ashes to Ashes* it is clearly negative. Although both plays have the same theme, the emotional charge changes because the message is different in each one.

Exercise 21

Consider the underlying theme and message of your scene – even a short scene will have both. Examine the behaviour of your characters and determine whether it is consistent with both their character and your theme and message. Check that your ending is consistent.

During the course of the story the protagonist has to undergo a change, either external or internal. Even if, at the end, they appear to be the same as at the start of the play, there should have been an emotional journey which has left its mark.

The audience, too, should have undertaken an emotional journey. How they will feel at the end of the play is down to the writer – but if the play has been well written the emotions they leave the theatre with will be the ones the writer intended.

Choices

In order to resolve conflict, people make choices. At every point of crisis in a story, the protagonist will have to make a choice, and the further into the plot the less predictable the choice will be. If the protagonist's reaction to the inciting incident is to shrug and walk away, then the story is over and there is no play. The audience knows this, and has the expectation that early in the play the protagonist will choose to accept the challenge that life has thrown at them. With each subsequent choice, however, there are more and more options open to the protagonist, but also there is much more at stake. Once the crisis is reached, the protagonist makes a choice that is irrevocable and must lead to the resolution – all the other options are closed down and the ending becomes inevitable.

Conflict in depth

You already know from Chapter 03 that conflict is part of character creation and from Chapter 05 that it is essential to a story. Conflict arises when a person desires something that, for whatever reason, they cannot have. The more extreme the desire, and the barriers to achieving that desire, the more dramatic possibilities there are in the story.

We know that as the plot unfolds the level of conflict needs to increase, building towards the moment of crisis where it looks as though all is lost. Now we need to look at conflict in more detail. Conflict can operate on one or more of three levels:

- internal conflict
- interpersonal conflict
- external conflict.

Internal conflict

A protagonist who is struggling with their inner demons has internal conflict. For this to work there have to be two conflicting characteristics, such as an obsessive career-driven person who also puts a high value on family life, or a good-time girl who has a serious side, or a paedophile trying to lead a moral life. While the novel is the prime art form for exploring inner conflict, it can be done very well on stage.

The difficulty lies in conveying to the audience the conflicting aspects of the protagonist's nature. This can be done in two ways:

- through soliloquy, where a character speaks their inner thoughts aloud without other characters overhearing
- by showing how the protagonist interacts with other characters chosen for their strong contrasts, which bring out the opposing sides of the protagonist's nature.

Case study: internal conflict

In *A Taste of Honey* by Shelagh Delaney, we see different sides of the protagonist Jo's personality according to whether she's with her mother, her lover or her male friend. With her mother she is abrasive and confrontational, with her lover she is hesitantly sexual and with her male friend, because she believes him to be gay, she feels able to show her doubts and insecurities.

Interpersonal conflict

This is conflict between the protagonist and one or more other people. Again, there has to be a disparity between the protagonist's desire and that of the other characters. This is the area where the majority of plots operate, because it is something we can all connect with. Whether it's a teenager who wants more freedom, a mother whose children won't behave, or an accounts clerk who dreams of escaping to Tahiti, we all know what it's like to feel our desires thwarted by other people.

External conflict

Here the protagonist, or group of protagonists, is in conflict with society at large. They may be actively in conflict, such as freedom fighters, eco-warriors or suffragettes, or passive victims of some social ill, but it is always society rather than their own nature or other people that is causing the problem. The difficulty with this type of story can be that losing the human element also weakens the audience's empathy with the characters. The answer to this is to tell the wider story through the experiences of a small group of people, who are living, breathing characters rather than ciphers.

Case study: external conflict

The Long and The Short and The Tall by Willis Hall depicts the realities of war and the brutal decisions which have to be taken. By reducing the conflict to seven soldiers who are faced with killing a Japanese prisoner of war, the writer brings the action down to a human level, making it easier for the audience to empathize with the characters' dilemmas.

Conflicts united

All stories will tend to contain elements of all three types of conflict, but with one type dominating. As much as anything, this is to do with audience expectation – the audience for a domestic drama will not expect to find themselves struggling to understand a political play, or an angst-ridden internal monologue. However, your play will be stronger if it includes something of all three levels of conflict.

Case study: conflicts united

Even a simple play like *Whatever You Want* demonstrates the three levels of conflict. Margaret's internal conflict is that she wants material possessions and a certain type of lifestyle, but is not quite ruthless enough to achieve wealth. Her interpersonal conflict is with her husband Ray, who never does what she wants him to do. Her external conflict is with the small town she lives in, because she isn't accorded the social status she feels she deserves. Although the external conflict was developed in early drafts of the play, we cut most of it in later versions – and we still aren't sure if that was the right thing to do.

Top tip

Choose a play you have seen recently and examine it for all three levels of conflict.

Exercise 22

Examine the three levels of conflict for your protagonist(s). Are they resolved? If not, can you see a way to resolve them?

Analogies

An analogy is a way of understanding something by using comparisons. For instance, trying to explain to a sulky teenage boy why homework is important can be an uphill struggle. But if you use the analogy of his footballing hero who needs to go to training sessions so that he can be a star on the pitch it might begin to make sense, because homework is a bit like training.

There are various aspects of writing and understanding plays that use analogy to add depth and texture.

Imagery

Images (or metaphors and similes) are essential to all art. By comparing one thing with another, the artist enables the audience's understanding. When Wordsworth wrote 'I wandered lonely as a cloud' he was using the cloud image to convey his meaning, creating a picture of a person as solitary as a single cloud in the vast sky.

Images help to load language with layers of meaning, so that in only six words Wordsworth could establish an atmosphere of drifting solitude as well as the information that he was out alone walking – all ready for the moment when he sees the daffodils and his heart lifts.

In playwriting, imagery can be used directly or indirectly. Directly, a character could say 'I'm as lonely as a cloud.' Indirectly, the character could talk about enjoying the kind of weather where a clear sky has just one cloud in it, or could resist going out on a sunny day because they find it too cheerful.

Strictly speaking, all human communication proceeds by metaphor. If a person claims to be 'lonely' we have an understanding of that concept only through comparison, mainly with our own experience. This means that we are quite likely to misunderstand someone if they are describing something that is completely alien to our own experience. It also means that 'lonely as a cloud' is a metaphor built on a metaphor. For most writing purposes, however, it is sufficient to use the concept of metaphor in its narrower sense.

Case study: imagery

Throughout *Long Day's Journey into Night* Eugene O'Neill uses the image of fog. He introduces it through setting the play on a single foggy day, and then transfers the image to the emotional fog that the family live in, and the mental fog that the mother struggles with because of her drug addiction.

Symbolism

An image becomes a symbol if it carries with it a meaning from outside the artwork. So, as well as giving a picture of Wordsworth's solitariness, the cloud might also be said to symbolize unhappiness, through its association with bad weather.

Symbolism in plays can operate in different ways through:

- language
- action
- setting
- props.

The key in each case is not to be too heavy handed. Once an audience has spotted the symbolism at work, all is lost. Keep it subtle but also accessible.

Some symbols are centuries old and well-established across many cultures – such as the idea that mountain peaks are sacred places because they take you closer to the gods. Others are more culture specific, such as the Union Jack as a symbol of British patriotism, or of British Imperialism, depending on your cultural bias.

> **Top tip**
>
> Symbolism will operate whether the writer intends it or not. If you set your play on a mountain top, or hang a Union Jack on the wall, it will mean something to the audience.

> ### Case study: symbolism
>
> *Dancing at Lughnasa* by Brian Friel is a prime example of the use of symbolism to reinforce both the themes and the character development of a play. For example, the survival of Ireland's pagan past is symbolized by a broken mirror, which will bring seven years bad luck if they don't keep the pieces. Dancing is also seen as an anarchic pagan activity and is therefore disapproved of by Kate, the most deeply Christian character. These are just two examples from a play loaded with symbolism.

Structured images and symbols

Working with images in a structured way creates a powerful tool for increasing the texture of your play. The structure can be:

- external – that is, using universally understood symbols
- internal – that is, a system developed just for that play.

Both images and symbols will feed through into the subtext of a play which is why they work so well when done with a subtle touch.

The idea is to create a set of images that can be woven into the play at all levels, but which is done so subtly that the audience is barely aware of it. Supposing you chose the weather as your image system, obviously you could specify thunderstorms (through sound effects) or sunlight (through lighting) to set the mood of different scenes. Characters could use weather-based imagery in their language 'I feel like a wet weekend' or 'he's like a little ray of sunshine'. Props could include an umbrella or a deckchair.

None of this sounds very subtle, but it all depends on how you do it. If someone uses the umbrella to murder the 'little ray of sunshine' character, then the image system begins to come to life.

Alternatively, you can create an image system that is unique to your play. A character could associate something – pink ribbon for example – with their long dead mother. Because of this they like to wear pink ribbon in their hair. If, by the end of the play, they have moved on from their obsession with losing their mother, they would discard the pink ribbon. Or if they suddenly discovered that their mother was still alive and had actually abandoned them, then the pink ribbon could be trampled in the dirt. If the character who will bring them this news is the one who accidentally spoils the ribbon, then that action will foreshadow the news that they are carrying.

Top tip

Analysing symbols and imagery is easier for most of us on the page – read a play script and analyse it for symbolism and structured imagery. Remember this is not a precise art and every reader will find different interpretations of a text.

Case study: image systems

In *Dancing at Lughnasa* Brian Friel develops a complicated image system of both internal and external symbols. The mirror and dancing are external symbols, but the broken radio is particular to this play. The radio is the source of the music that makes dancing possible, and its unreliability says something about the pagan world that it symbolizes – this, too, is unpredictable. There are many more images and symbols throughout the play creating a densely woven texture.

Plot as metaphor

Because images work by comparison it is possible to make your whole plot into an extended metaphor. If you see life as a journey, then a plot based on a journey could become a metaphor for life itself.

This is useful for writers who want to deal with a subject that is taboo or difficult in some way. There is nothing wrong with tackling it head on. You may find it hard to get the play produced, and if it is produced you may find the negative publicity distracts from the subject you're trying to pursue – although of course there is no such thing as bad publicity. Using an extended metaphor is simply an alternative.

Fairy stories are often no more than extended metaphors. *Sleeping Beauty*, for instance, is about sexual awakening and *Jack and the Beanstalk* is about a boy's passage through puberty to manhood. This explains their hold over us, and shows the power of this type of storytelling.

Plot as allegory

An allegory is a type of extended metaphor that has a strong moral purpose. At one time, allegory was a very popular way of conveying moral messages to a semi-literate society – *Pilgrim's Progress* by John Bunyan is a good example. During his journey through life, Bunyan's pilgrim meets various characters who personify all the virtues and vices, and who test him in various ways. This may seem an outmoded approach now, but it can still be used in a more subtle way. If you have a strong moral message to convey, then you will find that your play naturally turns into an allegory, with minor characters being used to stand for positive or negative aspects. It will work best if you spend some time fleshing them out – a modern audience won't respond if your characters are too one-dimensional.

Models

This is another way of looking at the underlying structure of a play, and is also a useful tool for a writer. It is based on the idea that in any group of people, individuals will tend to assume certain roles.

The most accessible model is probably the family, which almost everybody understands. You can apply the family model to almost any situation – an office, a school, a group of people on a coach trip. The model helps you understand how the interactions between various characters are fuelled. The child can be silly in ways that the adults can't. Siblings squabble, adults put a stop to it. Grandparents are indulgent, parents are stricter. It is effective to work against stereotype in the model, such as having an older character fill the role of child, while a younger one is an adult. Also consider having two members of a group, vying for the same role – both wanting to be the caring mother, or the authoritarian father.

Other types of model can also be used. For a political model ask yourself, is this group of characters a democracy or a dictatorship? Is there a power struggle going on? For a model from the natural world, ask is this a herd or a hunting pack? Is this character a rogue male gorilla being forced to cope with life in a co-operative ant's nest?

The model provides consistency and an underlying logic to behaviour that will help you work with your characters – but don't leave clues about it in the final script.

Case study: models

When we were writing *Whatever You Want*, everything became much clearer when we realized that for most of the scenes, Dilys was a child to Ray's easygoing father and Margaret's exasperated mother.

Work in progress

The suspense plot is driven by the unseen Mr Hubert and the failure of technology – the computer crashes, the printer starts to smoke. The emotional plot is driven by the two women and their different agendas. Beryl wants to get away from work and finish the task in hand. Mel wants to get away from work and make progress with Steve. None of the conflicts are resolved in this scene, because of the open ending. Mr Hubert represents Beryl's external conflict, and she has yet to deliver the figures to him. Her interpersonal conflict with Mel is ongoing, and her inner conflict between her desire to run things and her need to be liked is also not resolved. As the scene stands, the theme is frustration, but the underlying message isn't clear. Beryl needs to take responsibility for her situation. We pick the scene up near the end:

MEL: *(irritably)* For goodness sake, just click on that.

Mel and Steve exit. Beryl clicks the mouse, the printer makes a strange noise, smoke pours from it. The phone starts ringing.

BERYL: *(calling)* Mel, Steve, come back!

Beryl takes a fire extinguisher and sprays the printer. She then picks up the phone.

BERYL: I'm sorry Mr Hubert, but the figures have gone up in smoke. I will deal with it in the morning … no, I have to leave now because I have a doctor's appointment.

Summary

In this chapter you have learnt:

- about the deeper issue of plotting
- to recognize clichés, themes, messages and emotional content
- more about conflicts.

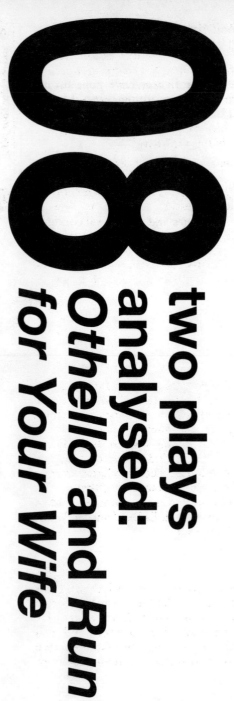

08

two plays analysed: *Othello* and *Run for Your Wife*

In this chapter you will learn:
- how to analyse a play
- how to compare plays
- about the underlying similarities between tragedy and comedy.

The most common mistake that new playwrights make is: there's no drama! Conflict is the basis of drama! Very often, new writers are not able to identify the conflict, which lies at the heart of the narrative they want to write. They don't really know what their protagonist's 'question' is (and, quite often, they don't know who their protagonist is either!) What is the problem that their main character must wrestle with and resolve by the end of script? And who or what is going to stand in their way?

Abigail Davies, script editor and producer

Analysing the work of other playwrights can provide a shortcut to understanding how drama works. *Othello* is one of Shakespeare's great tragedies, first performed in 1604, while *Run for Your Wife* is Ray Cooney's long running farce, first performed in 1982. With a gap of nearly 400 years, and in entirely different genres, it's instructive to examine the differences and similarities between the two plays.

Plots in brief

Othello

Othello is a black man who has become a successful general in the Venetian army (Venice at the time was powerful and civilized). He marries Desdemona, a Venetian, without obtaining her father's permission, but since she agreed to the marriage the authorities take no action against him. He is immediately sent to Cyprus to deal with a threat of war, and takes his new wife with him. A soldier called Iago hates Othello and sets out to destroy him. He persuades Othello that Desdemona has been unfaithful with Cassio, another soldier. Othello becomes mad with jealousy and kills Desdemona. When he realizes his mistake, he kills himself.

Run for Your Wife

John Smith is a mild-mannered London taxi driver who has married two women, and who lives a double life between two south London flats just a few minute's drive apart. He intervenes in a mugging, is hurt and taken to A&E, and as a result his carefully balanced schedule for running the two marriages falls apart. As he tries to restore normality he finds himself creating a pyramid of lies, mainly because two policemen have become interested in the mugging and the confusion at the hospital over his address. His shiftless neighbour Stanley tries to help him but ends up making matters much worse, until eventually John is forced to confess the truth.

Settings

The first act of *Othello* is set in Venice, the rest of the play takes place in Cyprus. Venice represents the control and balance of civilization but in Cyprus, which is on a war footing, anarchy takes over. In the alien environment of Cyprus the small number of Venetians are forced to interact with each other, creating a claustrophobic intensity. The environment is closed in the sense that it is an island.

Run for Your Wife takes place in the two flats, which are both represented on stage in a dual set. John Smith's homes are both claustrophobic for him since both his wives have taken the day off work, and because of the various outsiders who come to the front doors.

Characters

- Othello
- Iago
- Desdemona.

Othello gives his name to the play and would seem to be the protagonist, although there is a case for saying that Iago is the more interesting character who occupies more of the audience's attention. Desdemona is the third side of the triangle of three dominant characters. The contrasts between the three are strongly marked. Othello is powerful, open and honest, where Iago is sly and devious. Desdemona is virtuous but without any power, her happiness is in the hands of the men around her and particularly her husband Othello. Othello's tragic flaw is that he is too trusting and therefore easily manipulated by Iago.

- John Smith
- Stanley Gardner
- Mary Smith
- Barbara Smith.

John Smith is clearly the protagonist of *Run for Your Wife,* and Stanley is his sidekick. John's main relationship in the play is with Stanley. His wives have less importance than Desdemona, Mary Smith is a nice ordinary woman, and Barbara Smith, the second wife, is similar but more overtly sexual. However, they still form the third side of the triangle because without the wives there would be no story.

Minor characters represent the forces of society, whether it is Desdemona's father Brabantio in *Othello*, or the two policemen in *Run for Your Wife*.

Othello and John

Both protagonists are respectable members of society, and their respectability is important to them, and yet both are hiding something that threatens to undermine their respectability. Othello's strong passions are held in check by his civilized values, but when Iago manipulates him into sexual jealousy he loses all control, firstly by falling into a fit, then by abusing his wife, and finally by killing her. John Smith values his respectability so highly that he is prepared to tell any number of lies to preserve it. His secret, too, is sexually based.

The protagonists are overly concerned with preserving their reputation in both plays. Othello can't bear the shame attached to having an unfaithful wife, and John, who has two faithful wives, is determined to conceal his bigamy. Although we can't now fully understand the significance of fidelity in Shakespeare's time, we can be sure that many wives were unfaithful, and most didn't die as a result even then, so Othello was clearly overreacting to what he saw as social disgrace. We can be sure that in John Smith's day there were men who managed to marry one woman and maintain a relationship with another, without committing bigamy and without worrying about their reputation.

Stanley and Iago

Both plays demonstrate a problem that bedevils many dramas – an off-centre focus of interest. There is no doubt that for much of *Othello* wicked Iago is more interesting than virtuous Othello. The interest only switches to Othello when he starts to lose control. Similarly, feckless Stanley is more interesting and amusing than conventional John.

Desdemona, Mary and Barbara

In both plays the women are powerless. Desdemona is trapped by her own goodness – it simply never occurs to her that she not only needs to be virtuous, but to be seen to be virtuous. Mary and Barbara are both victims of John's bad behaviour, and it doesn't occur to either of them to be suspicious of him.

Plots in depth

Binding ties and what's at stake

In both plays the most important binding ties are those of marriage, although *Othello* includes the ties of military service and *Run for Your Wife* includes those of friendship.

Clearly there is much at stake in both plays. In *Othello* the risk initially centres around Othello's reputation, but eventually Desdemona's life and other lives are also threatened. John Smith is also risking social disgrace and eventually prison. However, this is barely mentioned – the lighter touch needed for comedy means that it is enough that an audience can be expected to know that bigamy is illegal.

Social and cultural background

Othello's different nature is a key aspect of the play and a theme of enduring interest. Like ET or Crocodile Dundee, Othello is making his way in an alien culture. He has been spectacularly successful and has taken on many positive Venetian values – however he has failed to understand the duplicity and manipulation that were the negative side of that culture.

Run for Your Wife explores exactly the opposite idea. All of the characters come from the same cultural background and apparently share the same values – John's secret is that he has broken the rules. This in itself makes John different from the people around him.

Vices and virtues

In both plays the back-story includes an immoral act by the protagonist. Othello has already eloped with Desdemona and married her – the opening scenes concern her father's outrage when he discovers this, and his demands that Othello be punished. John has already committed bigamy. Although both are basically good men, in each case one mistake sets off the chain that leads to their downfall.

Iago is chillingly evil and appears to have no virtues whatsoever. In his determination to destroy Othello he is prepared to commit murder. At first Iago tries to arrange for the killings to be done by Roderigo (a minor character whom he easily controls), but eventually he himself kills Roderigo and then his own wife Emilia. In this respect he resembles John Smith – like the protagonist of a farce, Iago has to go to greater and greater extremes as his plotting becomes more convoluted and closer to being discovered. However, Stanley is the true parallel for Iago. Where Iago works against Othello, Stanley works for John. Both characters become more and more deeply embroiled, and in neither case does the audience understand their motivation.

Although Iago gives reasons for hating Othello, they are unconvincing and disproportionate to the revenge he takes. At the end of the play he is arrested but still refuses to explain himself – he is led off to be tortured, leaving the audience convinced he will never talk. Without motivation Iago becomes a much more terrifying character – a psychopath against whom no normal person would have any defence. In the case of Stanley, we never really know why he goes to so much trouble to help John, although we can make deductions based on his character. He is work-shy, but, like a lot of lazy people, will go to great lengths when his interest is engaged. There is a mischief-making aspect to Stanley too, so that he seems to quite enjoy the power he has to drop John in it at any moment, and also there may be an element of male solidarity in his behaviour.

Parallelism

Both plays have a suspense plot and an emotional plot. Iago drives the what-happens-next plot of *Othello*, while it is Othello who takes the emotional journey from sanity to madness (this is why, ultimately, Othello is the true protagonist). Farce is often thought to consist entirely of what-happens-next, but there is an emotional plot, as John gradually realizes that his position is untenable, and as Mary and Barbara both become increasingly distressed by the strange behaviour of John and Stanley. The emotional charge of *Othello* is strongly negative, while *Run for Your Wife* is a mixture, i.e. it is ironic.

Set-up and exposition

Shakespeare dedicates the whole of Act I to the set-up and exposition of *Othello*. It takes place in Venice and sets everything up ready for the transition to Cyprus and the real action of the play. That is not to say the act is boring – it opens with the breaking news of the elopement and moves swiftly to the father's anger and demand for retribution. Note that Shakespeare uses an uninformed character in Act I Scene I – Roderigo has been wooing Desdemona and Iago tells him that she has married Othello. The technique works because Roderigo is an integral part of the plot, and also because we are able to see how Iago manipulates him. The rest of the Act allows us to see Othello in his prime (when he eloquently defends his action in eloping) and also the high esteem that the Venetian Senate holds him in.

Ray Cooney's set-up and exposition is far more complex. In the opening moments we see both wives phoning different police stations to report their husbands missing. Again the writer is using an uninformed character to give the audience information, but this time the audience neither hears nor sees them as they are at the other end of a telephone. The unusual dual set means that we can see both flats simultaneously, and the carefully structured one-sided dialogues as each woman talks into her phone set up the parallels between their lives. The two dialogues raise a suspicion that they may be talking about the same man, but this is not confirmed until some minutes into the play when John confesses to Stanley. It is a masterly example of how little exposition is needed when it is cleverly introduced.

Obstacles and twists

It is Iago who encounters the obstacles in the plot of *Othello*, which is another reason why he can appear to be the protagonist. He tells lies to Roderigo, Cassio, Desdemona and Othello to persuade them to do what he wants – at any point he could be discovered if the people concerned talk openly to each other, but he relies on his knowledge of each individual's psychology to stop that happening.

The same is true of John Smith, who is constantly in the position of telling an easy lie to one person which then has to be repeated and embroidered to another. By the end of the play most of the characters are on stage, all believing different things about each other and yet, because nobody speaks openly, none of the lies are discovered.

Being a farce, *Run for Your Wife* has far more twists than *Othello*. Because the characters move about within each flat and between the flats, and because they make phone calls, the plot is constantly turned in different directions.

Crisis and obligatory moment

Both plays have a crisis scene in the dead centre of the plot. In *Run for Your Wife* this comes at the end of Act I, and is correctly placed to make sure the audience return to their seats eager for Act II. John Smith has moved from one of his flats to the other, only to find himself confronted by the policeman who took him home from casualty to the first flat. We have to wait till Act II to see how he will explain his presence in the second flat.

The crisis in *Othello* is in the middle of Act III where it can have nothing to do with creating suspense for the audience across the interval, but everything to do with the rising dramatic arc. In this scene Desdemona accidentally drops the fancy embroidered handkerchief that Othello has given her. Iago keeps it and hides it in Cassio's lodgings so that it looks as if Desdemona has been there.

There is a clear cut and terrible obligatory moment in *Othello*, when Othello realizes that not only has he murdered an innocent woman, but that she has tried to save him by lying with her last breath (she claims to have killed herself) and will therefore spend eternity in Hell. John Smith has a far less dramatic obligatory moment, but when both his wives become quite hysterical, their distress seems to trigger him into confessing.

Climax and resolution

From the crisis, *Othello* moves inexorably towards its climax. Othello kills Desdemona and when it is too late he discovers her innocence. *Run for Your Wife* also moves inexorably towards its climax, in which John confesses to the policemen. The fact that his two wives are off-stage at the time, does not detract from the climactic moment as John is having to own up to his criminal behaviour to officers of the law – he could be arrested and lose everything.

The resolution in *Othello* comes when Othello kills himself. For John there is anti-climax and no resolution, since when he finally tells the truth he isn't believed.

Catharsis and conflict resolution

Clearly the emotional rollercoaster that is *Othello* will create catharsis in an audience, especially as there is an awful, poignant moment when Othello convinces himself that Desdemona is still alive. Othello's conflicts are only resolved when he dies.

John Smith's conflicts are never resolved and there is no catharsis in the content of the ending. However, the pause after his confession, followed by the final line 'You lying bastard' should create a huge laugh – and laughter is cathartic.

Themes and messages

The major themes in *Othello* are the difference between appearance and reality, and the gullibility of virtuous people. *Run for Your Wife* also explores, in a comedic way, the willingness of people to believe lies. Both plays examine the rules of civilized societies and show the price of breaking them. The message in both cases would seem to be that the rules are there for a reason, and breaking them only causes trouble.

Imagery and symbolism

As you would expect, *Othello* is saturated with powerful imagery and symbolism. Othello's blackness is contrasted with Desdemona's whiteness, and there are constant dark/light contrasts. The handkerchief assumes enormous importance and becomes a symbol of fidelity. Othello and Iago both use imagery in their speeches, and there is a strong contrast between Iago's animal coarseness and Othello's sophisticated beauty.

Imagery can be used in comedy, but in the case of *Run for Your Wife* there is very little of it – instead there is a running gag that builds throughout the play. Stanley's surname is Gardner and quite early on John lies to Barbara that Stanley is a farmer. This leads to a series of agricultural jokes built largely round the fact that neither John nor Stanley know anything about farming.

Conclusion

Why is *Othello* a tragedy and *Run for Your Wife* a farce? It is because the playwrights have told us that they are by the way they have written them. In real life bigamy is not funny, it is a tragedy. The lies and the betrayals are devastating, but by using the lightest of touches Ray Cooney finds the comedy in the situation. Conversely, with a re-write, *Othello* could make a brilliant black comedy. A man driven mad by jealousy when he has no cause is funny as long as he doesn't kill his wife, and as long as the mistake is caused by a series of misunderstandings rather than evil manipulation.

By comparing two such contrasting plays we have shown that tragedy and comedy are two sides of the same coin and require the same basic construction to be successful. Both these plays have stood the test of time, for the simple reason that they work on stage, practically, emotionally and psychologically.

You can use similar techniques to analyse your own work. You will be able to see whether it satisfies all the dramatic criteria or if there are any weak spots.

Summary

In this chapter you have learnt:

- that the underlying structure of Shakespeare's plays is still in use today
- that tragedy and comedy are two sides of the same coin.

09

keeping going, re-writes and polishing

In this chapter you will learn:
- how to finish a first draft
- how to approach re-writes
- about polishing
- how to receive feedback.

Remember how many plays and novels and movie scripts have been rejected, over and over again, before striking a chord with one individual, and going on to make millions! Award-winning veteran playwright Peter Nichols has 40 – yes, 40! – plays in his bottom drawer, all rejected! He still writes every day, undaunted...

Tony Staveacre, writer/producer in television, radio and theatre, author of three books on popular culture

Keeping going

Writer's block

Everybody has heard about writer's block. It is the dreaded moment when the writer sits staring at a blank piece of paper or computer screen, and cannot think of a word to write. In fact, we don't believe that writer's block exists. There are writer's tiredness, writer's poor attention span and writer's reluctance to make big changes – but no block. Often, all that is necessary is to prime the pump to get the creative flow started.

Reading this book, and following the exercises, will give you the skills to access what is buried in the back of your mind. However, there are some practical solutions for maintaining the flow:

- When you finish a writing session make a note to yourself of what you need to do at the start of the next session. This will make it easier to pick up from where you left off.
- Spend some time getting to know your characters – write something for them, in their voice, that is not part of the play. It could be a letter, or a phone call, or a short dialogue. Even their shopping list will tell you something about them. When you take the pressure off yourself like this, often the words start to flow.
- Spend some more time analyzing your story, look at its structure and examine the underlying themes.
- Turn the whole thing on its head, and imagine how the play would work if the protagonist made a different decision at the crucial moment. Don't worry if the result is something comically ludicrous, laughter is mentally refreshing and the new perspective on your play will help you find solutions to plot problems.
- Add another character or even get rid of one.

- If your play is based on real events or characters, more research into the subject could get you back on track.
- Remember, it is not essential to write your play from the beginning and work through to the end. Sometimes it is easier to write the end first and work backwards. Or start in the middle and go in both directions. There are no rules about this, every writer finds their own answers.

If you have solved all the practical problems with the play, and you still feel stuck, then look for answers outside of the play you are working on.

Try letting your subconscious do the work for you:

- Use relaxation techniques.
- Soak in a hot bath and let your mind wander.
- Do something physical like taking a brisk walk.

We know one writer who volunteers to do the family ironing at such times. Whatever method you choose don't consciously think about your problem, but let it be there, on the periphery, and see what pops up from your subconscious. Keep the notebook handy though.

Perhaps you need to re-energize yourself. There are various ways of doing this:

- We all know that listening to a motivational speaker can be inspiring, but so can going to see a play or reading a script.
- Joining a writer's group, particularly one specializing in plays, can provide the stimulus to keep you going. Writing, in the main, is a solitary occupation and meeting with like-minded people allows you to discuss what you are doing and the problems you may be encountering. You may find that suggestions made by other writers are often clever but wrong for your play – you realize at once that another voice is intruding into your dramatic world. This is just as helpful as suggestions which are pertinent, because the realization can be enough to put you back on track.
- Start a writer's group if you can't find one. You may be surprised at how many people there are out there writing plays and all wanting to get in touch with other playwrights.
- Check the Internet. There are several websites which allow writers to download their plays for criticism by other writers (see Taking It Further).

Finally, don't panic. Remember, your mind is a powerful organ and somewhere in there your play is waiting for you.

Writer's displacement activities

Of course there are lots of psychological reasons for not getting down to writing. Some writers find they cannot settle until all the distractions, such as cleaning the house, servicing the car, mowing the lawn, are out of the way. Others prefer to get their writing done at the start of the day and then mow the lawn, etc. Some writers can work in a noisy atmosphere such as a table in a café; others have to have complete silence in a shed at the bottom of the garden. Do whatever works for you, but don't make doing the chores or not having a room of your own an excuse for not writing. That's when they become displacement activities.

Top tip

The clue to identifying a displacement activity is when a trivial task suddenly assumes a tremendous importance. Make a note to do it later and carry on writing.

Stamina

Writing a play takes a lot of mental stamina and there is always a point somewhere along the road where you feel like giving up. How many people have got a half-written script in the desk drawer or on their hard disc that has long been abandoned? Don't be one of them. Keep going until you get to the end of your first draft. It doesn't matter if some parts are more fully written than others.

On the whole, successful writers treat writing like a job, even if it has to be a part-time one. Write something five days a week, and have a two-day break. Get into a rhythm and keep on piling up the words. Remember, it's a draft, so it doesn't have to be perfect. The more you write, the more you will develop the stamina to keep on writing.

> **Top tip**
>
> If there is a scene that feels too challenging to write, or that is blocking your progress, just make a note as to what it should contain and move on to the next scene.

Take a break

Once you have reached the end of the first draft, put it away safely or take a backup, and then take a break. You will be tired, maybe relieved, hopefully exhilarated – you need to let that all subside before you go back to the play. Professional writers will always have another writing project they can turn to, but if you haven't, don't worry – think of all those odd jobs that have been neglected while you were writing. Immerse yourself in something else and let your mind clear.

Re-writes

After a break of a week or two it is time to re-write the play.

- Start by reading it all the way through. If anything leaps out at you as needing attention, make a note of it and keep reading – you need to get a feel for the complete piece, so don't get sidetracked into re-writing just yet.
- Your notes may well tell you where the most urgent need for re-writing lies, in which case you can deal with those problems first.
- After that it is important to go through the play in a systematic way, checking one aspect at a time.
- If you feel your concentration failing, take another break.

Drafts

How many drafts should you expect to write? More than you think – but there is no definitive number. A writer who is satisfied with their first draft is either a genius or a beginner. Expect to go through several versions of a play before you are happy with it. Each check needs to be done meticulously – and you can be sure that the one you are most reluctant to bother with is the one you really need to do.

Remember, not everything you write will be staged – there is a learning process to go through. But nothing is ever wasted – keep the best parts and recycle them and, if nothing else, you will appreciate the stamina needed to complete a piece of work. Then get straight on with writing the next play.

Polishing

Now is the time to ensure that everything is in place. One way is by using a system of checklists.

Check 1

- Theme
- Message
- Emotional charge.

Start by checking on these aspects of your play's deep structure. Analyse the three elements and make sure they all hang together. Although a theme can lead to any type of ending, the message and the emotional charge need to be in harmony with the ending. If you ever came away from a play scratching your head and wondering what it was all about, you can be sure the writer failed to carry out this check.

Check 2

- Basic plot
- Detailed plot
- Ask awkward questions.

Summarize your plot in a sentence, and then in a paragraph. Finally, write a synopsis of the plot as if you were trying to sell it to a theatre producer. Then play devil's advocate and ask yourself if it is interesting, exciting or funny enough to persuade the public to pay for tickets and sit through the performance. If the answer is no, then you have some serious restructuring to do.

One you have achieved the correct broad sweep in the plot, it is time to look at the details. Write out a detailed step-by-step breakdown of your plot. Try to stand outside of your involvement with it and examine it for holes. Ask the most awkward questions you can think of. Are the ties binding the characters strong enough to keep them together? Is there enough at stake to keep the protagonist going to the bitter end? If there is information that one character has and another doesn't, ask yourself if it is reasonable for the first character to keep it to themselves. What is their reason for keeping quiet? Would the second character ask them about it? Go through all the aspects of your plot in this way, challenging and questioning them.

Check 3

- Character consistency
- Audience assumptions.

Now is the time to go back to your original concept of the characters and see how much they've changed. Write out new notes for each character incorporating any changes, and then check that you have applied them consistently. It is very easy, in a first draft, to change a character as you get into the writing. For instance, you may come to realize that, several scenes in, the plot is helped along if a certain character is rather irritable. This is fine, but you need to either go back to the beginning and establish them as irritable before the scene where it is needed, or else to show why in that particular scene they would suddenly become irritable.

It is particularly important to look at moments when characters appear to step out of their stereotype. Remember, the audience is bound to make assumptions about your characters based on their early appearances. When you take the character out of the stereotype it begins to really come to life, but the character must remain both convincing and consistent.

Check 4

- Dialogue.

It is common for a writer to give characters too much to say. This is often because the writer is using the dialogue to make notes for themselves regarding what information they want to give the audience. Now is the time to weed out all those extraneous words. Where there is information in a speech, ask yourself how necessary it is, and cut it if it is not absolutely essential.

Check 5

- Voice consistency
- Vocabulary.

Next look at each character's speeches in isolation – read them out loud, or, if possible, have someone read them to you. This check is not about the content of the speeches, which you have already firmed up through looking at plot, character and information, but the voice. The greatest danger is that every character will speak in your voice and not theirs, so check for that. Reading your words out aloud also shows you whether the dialogue is actually sayable. Speeches often look wonderful on the page, but can be difficult for the actor to say.

Think of how each character would express the various emotions and reactions that the plot puts them through. If a character is surprised, do they say 'wow' or 'golly gum drops', or are they simply speechless? Remember, this draft is not about whether or not they are surprised, but about how they express it.

Go through every character in this way, even the most minor ones. It will add immeasurably to the texture and believability of your play.

Check 6

- Body language
- Business
- Stage directions.

These checks are almost always about cutting rather than expanding. When you are writing your early drafts you need to be able to see the play in your mind's eye, and inevitably you will write in all the actions, facial expressions and business with props. Now is the time for you to go through and cut all but the absolutely essential. In other words, leave room for the director and actors to add something to the play. By doing this you will make it more likely that your script is respected. If there are only a few directions then they are clearly important, if there are masses of them it just looks like you are being fussy.

Putting on a play is a group activity and if you trust your cast and crew they will almost certainly improve on your raw material.

Case study: actor's input

Here is a small moment from our sitcom *Adam 'n' Eve*:

EVE: Did I hear someone say... Cynthia? (*sobs*)

STUART: Now look what you've done. (*to Eve*) Let it all out, OK?

EVE: Yes, yes, I must, mustn't I?

ADAM: Hey, we're all sad. She was my aunty, remember? I mean, you've only lost a business partner, I've lost family. Wendy, doughnuts, chop chop, there's a good girl.

When we wrote this short dialogue it was about heartless Adam and our focus was on his speech at the end. In rehearsal the actor playing Stuart added some business – he picked up a box of tissues and passed one to Eve as he spoke, then another, then another – it was perfectly timed and raised a laugh on the night. More importantly, it underlined the contrast between Adam and soppy Stuart.

Check 7

• Murder your babies.

This is probably the hardest part of being a writer, so much so that the rather disturbing phrase 'murder your babies' has become the standard way of referring to what you need to do next. There will be some aspect of your play that you are really pleased with. It may be a character, a scene, or even a single line. Only you know what it is, but now you must look at it closely and ask yourself if it is really necessary. The fact that you are so pleased with it means that you haven't been looking at it objectively. Try taking it out, and see what happens. It's sad but true that more often than not the play is better without your favourite child. In fact, most of us find that early drafts of a play have more than one baby that needs removing.

One of the advantages of working with another writer is that the deed can be done for you. We ruthlessly cut out each other's favourites but we never throw them away. Time and again we have found that the baby isn't murdered after all – it's kept and used in another play.

Feedback

Before you ask for feedback, you need to examine your ego. If it is fragile, then only ask those people who will praise your work – your mum, your aunty, your best friend. If you think you can take it, then ask someone who will tell you the truth. These people can be surprisingly difficult to find. Ultimately you will send your script to a theatre, or enter it for a competition, both of which sometimes provide reader's reports (see Chapter 19), but before that you need a more informal sort of feedback. Ideally you need someone who is interested in the theatre, who has the courage to tell you the truth and who doesn't have an agenda of their own. In the real world, you will make do with what you can get. The more people you can ask, the better. Don't drive yourself mad trying to implement all their suggestions, rather look for the common denominators. If everybody thinks your protagonist is boring, or your plot doesn't make sense, then they are probably right.

Top tip

Never stop looking for feedback. If a play of yours is being performed, eavesdrop on the audience reaction in the interval – as long as no one recognizes you, you'll overhear the truth. When we put on our own production of *Over Exposure*, we tucked a short questionnaire into every programme. The comments were invaluable.

Ongoing changes

The script that you present to your director should be the best you can produce, but inevitably in rehearsal and performance you will realize that changes need to be made. In rehearsal particularly, this can lead to some difficult decisions. The director tells you something isn't working, or an actor complains they can't say a certain line, or they can't find their motivation. You should start by trying to explain fully what you intended, but supposing they still aren't happy? Should you ask them to dig deeper, and make your script work, or should you make the changes they want? Only you can decide, and it will come down largely to experience.

Once the play has been performed you may well see the need for other changes. Maybe the director and actors were right all along, or maybe the audience reaction shows you that something you all missed isn't working. This is why a play is often tried out in the provinces before it is taken to the West End – it not only ensures the performances are fully polished, it also gives the writer a chance to improve the script. All of our plays have been re-written following their first performances. Even well-established writers make major changes during the rehearsal process, in fact some regard it as an essential part of writing a play.

Exercise 23

Reading Chapter 08 will have given you the necessary break from your scene. Carry out the checks listed above and re-write it accordingly.

Work in progress

The scene now has a closed ending, but it needs a better resolution. By taking a break from the work it is easier to see one way of resolving the matter. If we add in the fact that the computer equipment is old it gives a better reason for the ending to be a closed one – the fault lies with Mr Hubert.

STEVE: *(to Mel)* No wonder it crashed, how many games have you downloaded?

MEL: Not that many.

STEVE: All this equipment needs updating, it came out of the Ark.

MEL: *(laughing)* Probably blow up one day.

Steve continues typing.

STEVE: Is that what you were working on?

He gets up and Mel sits down.

MEL: There you are Beryl, panic over. Thanks Steve, you're a honey.

STEVE: I aim to please.

BERYL: Could we just get this finished please?

The phone rings on Beryl's desk, she answers it.

BERYL: Yes Mr Hubert, I have them right here. *(She hangs up.)*

MEL: *(to Steve)* You off home then or do you fancy a drink?

STEVE: Could do.

They start to move off stage.

BERYL: You can't go yet. How do I print them off?

Mel comes back.

MEL: *(irritably)* For goodness sake, just click on that.

Mel and Steve exit. Beryl clicks, the printer makes a strange noise, smoke pours out of it. Phone starts ringing.

BERYL: *(calling)* Mel, Steve, come back!

Beryl takes a fire extinguisher and sprays the printer. She then picks up the phone.

BERYL: I'm sorry Mr Hubert, but the figures have gone up in smoke ... you will need to buy a new system ... no, I will deal with it in the morning ... I have to leave now because I have a doctor's appointment.

Summary

In this chapter you have learnt:

- that writer's block doesn't exist
- how every play needs more than one draft
- about the value of feedback.

section two

10 types of drama

In this chapter you will learn:
- about different types of drama.

The most common mistake that new playwrights make is: making the script too long, if it cannot be said in two hours perhaps it isn't worth saying. But practice makes perfect so work at it and listen to what people say about your work.

Sheila Hannon, creative producer, Show of Strength Theatre Company

When you picked up this book you probably already had an idea what sort of play you wanted to write, for what sort of performers and what sort of audience. Even so, it is worth taking a moment to consider the possibilities. Not every writer makes it in the West End, but there are plenty of other options that can provide a satisfying outlet for original work, and a useful training ground that may lead on to the professional heights.

By considering all types of drama you will greatly increase your chances of seeing your piece performed. As well as the satisfaction this brings it is also the best possible learning experience – nothing highlights your weaknesses as a writer better than watching an actor struggle to say your lines, or realizing that the audience has missed the point of the piece.

Genre

All art forms have genres. This simply means a work that conforms to a set of conventions. The conventions develop over a period of time, and the audience will come to a genre play with certain expectations. These conventions are useful to the writer, especially in exposition, which can be pared down because of the knowledge the audience brings to the performance.

The writer walks a fine line between obeying the conventions and fulfilling the audience expectations on the one hand, and avoiding stale old cliché on the other. Mostly the rules of genres have loosened over time, so that writers now have a fair amount of freedom within quite broad parameters.

If you want to write in a certain genre, there is no substitute for immersing yourself in it by watching performances and reading scripts. Pantomime and musicals, which have more extensive conventions than most other genres, are discussed in Chapters 13 and 14.

Genres covered:

- tragedy
- comedy
- light drama
- thriller
- historical
- experimental drama
- extemporized drama
- musicals
- pantomime
- religious drama
- adaptations
- children's plays
- monologues
- reviews and sketches.

Tragedy

For many people tragedy is the ultimate form of drama. Some writers feel that it's the only one worth attempting, while for others the size of the task is daunting. Shakespeare seems to dominate the field, and who can compete with him? The answer, of course, is not to try.

The classical idea of tragedy is that the protagonist is led to their ultimate downfall by some aspect of their own personality, and by the end of the play they achieve a full realization of what they have done. There are many variations on this basic theme, and although there is always an unhappy ending, it doesn't have to be a stage littered with dead bodies – a failed marriage, a wasted life, a lost cause, can all be tragedy.

Comedy

Stage comedy is not the same as stand-up or television sitcom. Stage comedy needs a strong setting, good characters and a story, however bizarre or surreal any or all of these might be. The strongest comedies show how the protagonist is led to their ultimate downfall by some aspect of their own personality – just the same as for tragedy. The difference lies in what is at stake. While Macbeth risked all for a kingdom, a comedy protagonist might risk only his respectability for a Mayorship. (See Chapter 11 for more on comedy writing.) Within comedy there are a range of subgenres.

- **Light comedy** includes romantic comedy and domestic comedy. Noel Coward excelled in light romantic comedies, such as *Blythe Spirit*, which are full of froth, witty one-liners and repartee, and generally end happily.
- **Satire** uses humour to criticize – a person, a society or an attitude. The writer appears to be agreeing with the concept being satirized, but the use of irony and sarcasm indicates the opposite. Examples are *Oh! What a Lovely War* by Charles Chilton and, from television, the final *BlackAdder* series set in the First World War.
- **Comedy of manners** holds up a section of society for ridicule, such as in *The Importance of Being Ernest* by Oscar Wilde.
- **Comedy thrillers** don't have to be as funny as a true comedy, and the thriller part is generally less frightening and graphic than a true murder mystery. A good example is *Ghost Train* by Arnold Ridley where a group of passengers are stranded on an eerie railway station and terrorized by a spectral train which turns out to be only too real and run by smugglers.
- **Farce** is characterized by a protagonist who has a secret and who is prepared to go to improbable lengths to protect that secret. Pure farce has been unpopular with critics in recent decades but audiences still turn out for it. Writers like Alan Aykbourn and Michael Frayn have used the farce format to produce high quality dramas. The keys to farce are that the protagonist must have something considerable at stake, and it must be played absolutely straight.
- **Parody** sets out to ridicule a genre. They can be humorous, such as the film *Blazing Saddles* which is a parody of cowboy films, or ironical such as *The Real Inspector Hound* by Tom Stoppard where he uses a parody of a country house murder mystery for his play-within-a-play.
- **Burlesque** is a form of parody which takes a popular fashion, especially a fashion in serious drama, as its topic.

Light drama

Rather out of fashion on stage, light drama has been largely taken over by films and television. This category includes romance and most family sagas. If you feel sure of getting an audience, then by all means write a light drama.

Thriller

Again, films and television have taken over the thriller, but a stage thriller can still grip an audience. The key is to have plenty of twists and turns in the plot, a few surprises, and an ending that sends your audience home intrigued but satisfied.

Historical

Some forms of historical drama just set out to give an audience an insight into what life was like in the past. While this is a valuable exercise, the best historical plays find a way to use the past to tell us something about the present. For instance, when Arthur Miller wrote *The Crucible*, which is ostensibly set in 1692, he was really writing about contemporary America. His play about seventeenth century witch-hunts was saying something about the McCarthy era, when society's obsession with the Communist threat caused similar destructive behaviour.

Experimental drama

Much loved by drama students, and always in evidence at the Edinburgh Fringe Festival, there is a place for drama that pushes the boundaries. Sometimes it works, and sometimes it doesn't. That's the whole point of the experiment.

Extemporized drama

This can be a difficult area for a writer to get into, since it involves the whole company working together to develop the play, but it can be extremely rewarding.

A major exponent of this type of drama is Mike Leigh who created *Abigail's Party,* a modern comedy of manners. When unhappily married couple Beverly and Lawrence invite their neighbours round for drinks, what starts as an evening of 1970s-style entertaining ends in tragedy.

Musicals

Musicals need a story just like any other play. In opera this is called the libretto, in musicals it's called the book, but in both cases somebody had to write it. See Chapter 14 for more information.

Pantomime

An endlessly popular genre for both amateur and professional groups. There is very little opportunity to develop original stories (although it does happen occasionally), but within the traditional plots a writer can create something of their own. See Chapter 13 for more information on writing pantos.

Religious drama

Drama and religion have always been closely linked. Most religions are based on a strong story, and carry elements of drama in their rituals and practices. For the writer, there may be opportunities to write drama for their local place of worship. It is very rare, however, for religious drama to achieve commercial success.

Adaptations

A highly specialized area of writing, but one that can be extremely rewarding. Currently very popular, recent years have seen West End adaptations of both films and books.

Children's plays

Plays for children to watch, rather than for them to perform in, are always popular. As well as commercial theatre, there are many small touring groups that take drama into schools, usually performing short pieces aimed at helping children understand difficult non-academic topics such as child abuse or bullying. While they often write their own material, you may find there is interest in your ideas if you have special knowledge of a relevant subject.

Monologues and one-woman or one-man shows

One character talks directly to the audience. This requires great discipline in the writing, and great talent in the performance.

Reviews and sketches

This is another form that is very popular with students, as the review gives everyone a chance to perform without having to carry a major role. Writing one or two short sketches for a review can be a great way of starting out, but beware, a sketch needs discipline and focus. Characters need to be instantly recognizable and there is no room for complicated set-ups.

Summary

You should now be able to:

- recognize the various genres
- decide on the type of play you want to write.

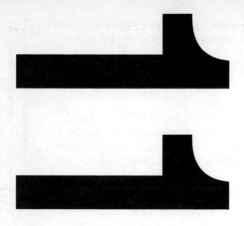

11

writing a comedy play

In this chapter you will learn:
- about the principles of comedy
- how to create comedy characters
- how to create comedy plots
- how to end a comedy.

The main thing I look for in a new script is: a new voice, and a story that grabs my attention on page one. A good joke helps, too.

Tony Staveacre, writer/producer in television, radio and theatre, author of three books on popular culture

There is always a demand for comedies. People like to laugh, and it's good for them – it has now been medically established that laughing can improve one's health. Comedy, more than any other form of drama, arises out of the relationship between the audience and the performance. The audience is a willing participant in the process of being amused and entertained.

Comedy began with the Greeks, who apparently produced quite obscene plays. The sexual references have come down through the ages via restoration comedies and farce with its double entendres.

In serious plays, humour can act as a counterpoint to a dramatic moment and be used to change the dynamics of a situation, but this is not true comedy.

There is a wide range of reasons for writing comedy. Some writers just want to create an uplifting experience for their audience; others have a deeply serious or polemical intent. All are equally valid.

- Some comedies are the reverse of tragedies – their plot lines are the same, but the writer indicates to the audience that it is alright to laugh.
- Some comedies have the tragic element so near the surface that even while laughing the audience will feel uncomfortable about it.
- Some writers believe that all comedies should include elements of sadness and that the audience's emotions should be constantly manipulated.
- Some plays start off as comedies and end as tragedies.

A serious business

Comedians and comedy writers are often quite solemn people who regard comedy writing as a serious business. When you first start writing comedy, you may find yourself laughing helplessly at your own jokes. There is nothing wrong with this, and you should always write in ways that you find funny. The hard work starts when that laughter wears off, and you have to re-write and polish material that has long since ceased to amuse you.

Jokes

Jokes are the least important part of a comedy. Jokes are for stand-up comedians, and if you have the knack of writing jokes there is always a market for them. In a drama, jokes are like the fancy ribbon on a parcel: they might make things look pretty but they have very little to do with the actual content.

Jokes can be a useful part of the preparation for writing a comedy. Once you know the main thrust of the play it is a good idea to spend some time writing down all the jokes and funny lines that come to mind around that topic. Also once you have created your characters, work out some jokes based around their interests and behavioural quirks. However much you love these jokes, accept that most of them won't find their way into the play. The exercise is aimed at getting you into the mood for writing comedy, exploring your plot and characters, and clearing your mind of all the jokes that crowd into it. As you start to write, you may well see places where a few of the jokes will sit beautifully – that is fine, but don't overdo it.

Remember that however wonderful a joke is, in the wrong place, or in the wrong play, it will have a disastrous effect. Comedy has a rhythm of peaks and troughs, and laughs feed off previous laughs. A wrongly placed joke can ruin that.

Comedy principles

- Incongruity
- Inversion
- Misunderstanding
- Double entendres
- Audience anticipation
- The informed audience
- Wordplay
- Bathos
- The mystery element
- Exaggeration
- Counting the laughs.

Incongruity

Laughter comes from the placing together of two ideas that don't belong together. This principle applies at every level of humour. A simple doctor-doctor joke is funny because the patient says something unexpected, not the sort of thing people normally say to a doctor. The doctor's response is equally incongruous, not the response you'd expect from a doctor:

PATIENT: Doctor, doctor, I keep thinking I'm a pair of curtains.
DOCTOR: Well sit down and pull yourself together.

When this principle is extended to a play, it is immediately obvious that comedy will come from a mixture of the bizarre and the mundane. You can have ordinary people grappling with a bizarre situation, or you can have bizarre people grappling with an ordinary situation – but you can't have bizarre people in a bizarre situation, or ordinary people in an ordinary situation.

So, a writer who creates a play about a group of eccentrics who decide to live an alternative lifestyle in a cave and who endure a series of weird mishaps will struggle to create laughs. However, if one of the characters is a totally conventional bank clerk who has mistakenly joined the venture thinking it was a holiday break, then there is potential for humour. Similarly, a single eccentric character placed in a deeply conventional situation (sent to work in the bank by a temping agency perhaps) will also generate comedy.

Inversion

A lot of comedy comes from turning things around or looking at them backwards, which is just another form of incongruity. A tiny woman who bosses her enormous husband around, or a useless football team whose coach sends them for ballet training, have the potential for comedy. Classic stories can be made funny by turning them upside down. How about Jill and the Beanstalk, or Romeo and Juliet retold with two older people whose grown up children disapprove of their relationship?

Misunderstandings

Misunderstanding is a simple way of setting up incongruity. It provides the conflict which drives the plot.

Case study: misunderstandings

In *Over Exposure*, family photographer Fred Fittleworth agrees to take some photos for a magazine called *Over Forty* believing it to be for women over the age of 40, when it is in fact a cheesecake magazine full of busty models. His initial misunderstanding is the hook that the plot hangs on.

Double entendres

Double entendre is a French phrase meaning 'double meaning' and in comedy it always signifies a smutty or obscene meaning hidden inside an apparently innocuous remark. Badly done it can create the effect of a school playground but cleverly done it always works well. If the play is for a family audience the double entendres will not be understood by the children, but will be enjoyed by the adults.

Audience anticipation

Much laughter is generated by an audience's anticipation. If the banana skin is in full view on the stage they will be waiting for someone to slip on it. They will laugh when various characters manage not to slip on it, and laugh again when finally somebody does slip. They will even laugh if someone picks it up and puts it in their pocket without anyone having fallen over. In the same way you can place metaphorical banana skins in the script; places where an audience can see a joke coming and anticipate it, but always try to add a twist that they weren't expecting.

The informed audience

Although it keeps an audience interested if a drama throws up unexpected twists, turns and shocks, there are occasions when the audience benefits from knowing something that one or more of the characters don't know.

Case study: the informed audience

In *Don't get your Vicars in a Twist*, through a series of misunderstandings, Marigold believes that Charles has had a vasectomy, although the audience knows that he had a boil on his neck. Because she is too delicate to say the actual word, and because Charles has no idea that Marigold is not referring to his boil, the following conversation is at cross purposes.

MARIGOLD: Did you have a general or a local anaesthetic?

CHARLES: An anaesthetic! No, I didn't have anything.

MARIGOLD: *(horrified)* Nothing! But didn't it hurt?

CHARLES: Too bloody right it did.

MARIGOLD: But that's appalling. Who did it for you?

CHARLES: No one, I did it myself.

MARIGOLD: *(even more horrified)* You did it yourself! Couldn't you afford to have it done properly?

CHARLES: I didn't want anyone to see it, it was so large.

MARIGOLD: Oh my word.

CHARLES: And the throbbing, it nearly drove me mad.

MARIGOLD: Good heavens. What did you do?

CHARLES: Well, I cauterized a knife on the gas stove and pierced it.

MARIGOLD: I think I'm going to faint.

CHARLES: I damn nearly fainted myself. But it did the trick. And it hardly left a scar, do you want to see?

MARIGOLD: Well, not here, later perhaps.

CHARLES: Look.

He pulls his collar down.

MARIGOLD: What are you talking about? I thought you'd had a vasectomy.

CHARLES: A vasectomy! No, I had a boil.

The main laugh comes at the end when Marigold realizes that all along Charles has been talking about a boil on his neck. However, because the audience knows in advance that Charles has had a boil not a vasectomy, every line then becomes a double entendre and creates a rising series of laughs as Marigold's imagination goes into overdrive.

Wordplay

A lot of humour comes from wordplay, but, like jokes, it can't be the dominant part of a play. It needs to arise from plot and/or character and it needs to be used in a rigorously disciplined way. The English language lends itself to wordplay because so many words sound the same but have completely different meanings.

Another type of word play relies on choosing the wrong words. The greatest example of this is Mrs Malaprop from *The Rivals* by Sheridan. This character aimed for a grand vocabulary but unfortunately constantly got it wrong. For example 'He is the very pineapple of politeness' (instead of 'pinnacle of politeness') and 'I'm sure I've done everything in my power since I exploded the affair' (instead of 'exposed the affair').

Case study: wordplay

In *Don't get your Vicars in a Twist*, the Bishop is still groggy after a blow on the head:

FREDA: Good heavens! That's even worse, what were you doing scrubbing Lady Alicia's back?

HERBERT: *(groggily coming round)* Pardon?

ANGELA: Lady Alicia's back.

HERBERT: Is she! Where's she been then?

ALAN: He's coming round.

GEORGE: Can I call you a taxi, Sir?

HERBERT: Of course you can. And what shall I call you?

Bathos

Bathos, or the move from the sublime to the ridiculous, is one of the staples of comedy. A play about an Emperor who believes himself to have divine powers might be mildly amusing, but a play about the owner of a pickle factory who has the same belief would be much funnier.

The mystery element

Nobody is quite sure why some things are funnier than others, except that it does seem to be both cultural and historical, and therefore the list changes all the time. The pickle factory mentioned above seems to be inherently funnier than a factory that makes car parts. A great aunt is a funnier relative than a second cousin. A tandem is funnier than a motorbike. And for some decades now the letter 'K' has been the funniest letter of the alphabet. When you are making your choices, therefore, pay some attention to these things, but don't let them dominate your thinking.

Exaggeration

This can be used to great effect in both characterization and dialogue. While not making the protagonist a caricature, a little exaggeration of their manners and foibles adds a comedic element. In the *Odd Couple*, both Oscar's slobbishness and Felix's obsessive tidiness have been exaggerated in order to increase the comedy value.

Similarly with dialogue, there is very little comedy if a character says, 'I've been waiting for several minutes for you'. But if they say, 'I've been waiting here for years. Look, I've taken root,' then it is funnier.

Counting the laughs

Beginners often feel that writing should be instinctive, and that applying any kind of system is somehow cheating. This seems to apply even more in comedy writing, where the writer often surfs a wave of inspiration, writing and chuckling to themselves as they do so. It's a wonderful feeling, but afterwards it is always a good idea to go back over the script and count the laughs. Mark each one in some way. A rule of thumb for a full-blown comedy is that each page of the script should have three verbal laughs and two physical laughs. That is a lot, but it is good discipline to try to achieve it, and you will be surprised how much more laughter you can squeeze out of your script.

They do not, of course, have to all be comedy peaks creating huge laughter. In fact, the play would be less effective if it was structured with only big laughs. Don't despise the weaker laughs, they are part of the rhythm of comedy. An audience needs to be led up to the big laughs, and carried down the other side of them with smaller moments of comedy.

Settings

There is nothing inherently funny about any setting. *The Entertainer* by John Osborne is about a music hall performer, and yet it is a deeply sad play. Hospitals are places of disease and death, and yet many comedies have been set in medical situations. In fact, the principle of incongruity suggests that there would be more humour in a hospital than in the life of a comedian.

Once you have chosen your setting, look for the humour potential in it. Think about people's real-life experiences in that setting and exaggerate them, or turn them on their heads. Humour from the setting is not essential. In *Over Exposure*, our setting was an empty flat and all of the comedy came from the characters and plot.

Characters

Character flaws

Greed, lust, stupidity, thoughtlessness – it is the character's own flaws which precipitate the situations in which they find themselves and which generate the humour.

Case study: character flaws

In *Over Exposure*, greed kicks in when Fred finds out the true nature of the magazine, because he wants the money to pay for his campaign to become Mayor. He decides to go ahead with the photo shoot in the hopes that his puritanical wife won't find out. This sets off a chain of events which sees him dressing up as his own sister and fighting off the amorous advances of a European Union bureaucrat.

Dialogue and speech patterns

Comedy in dialogue arises out of the characters. A slow-thinking person who can't keep up with a quick-witted one is funny, especially if the slow person has the last laugh. A strong regional accent can be made funny by a good actor. Speech habits such as catchphrases are funny if used carefully. Misinterpretations precipitate misunderstandings, create double entendre and can also be funny in themselves.

Case study: speech patterns

In *Over Exposure*, one of the characters is a German who has a sketchy grasp of English:

HANS: You are shooting the special lady, that is the murder.

LEN: No, no, he's not shooting her, he's shooting her *(beat)* with a camera.

HANS: Oh I see. Now I can relieve myself.

This gave us a few opportunities for laughs, and of course double entendres, but the possibilities increased enormously when we decided that Hans enjoyed copying English accents:

HANS: I am hearing Vic on phone *(he puts one hand to his ear, attempting a Cockney accent)* "Ere John, I want that special model again, y'know, enormous jugs, no brain? Bung 'er round to Frederick Fittleworth's Photographic today. Twelve o'clock sharp.'

Relationships and body language

Most of the humour in a play will come from the way the characters interact with each other. Remember the principle of incongruity, and apply it to the relationships. Always indicate how a character reacts to something – a good actor will develop laughs from reactions.

Body language, too, can be enormously funny. Physical humour has an important place in comedy but it must not be allowed to turn into slapstick – that is the prerogative of pantomime. Remember that not all actors can cope with physical comedy, so it's best to confine it to one or two of the roles, so that actors can be cast who have the necessary ability.

Plot

Comedies follow exactly the same rules as straight drama: there has to be a set-up, trigger and payoff and conflict is the driving force.

The core of your plot doesn't have to be funny in itself. *Over Exposure* is about a man who needs money to finance his bid to become Mayor of his town. He wants to do this because he feels the town has tended to look down on him. This could be a straight play. However, your developed plot should be funny. Imagine you are telling someone the story of the play in a few sentences, and see if it is amusing. Don't worry if it is not side-splittingly funny, but the plot should contain some basic humour as the foundation of the play.

Don't forget the dramatic arc. The peaks and troughs of dramatic arcs in comedy are marked by laughter. The biggest laughs should always placed at the moment of crisis, with smaller laughs during the build-up and afterwards.

Act I should not only end with an unresolved crisis, but that crisis should precipitate one of the biggest laughs of the act. It should also leave the protagonist in a situation that is going to be difficult to resolve.

Case study: Comedy dramatic arc

At the end of Act I of *Over Exposure* Fred is caught by the Brussels bureaucrat, wearing a wig and dress and trying to photograph a scantily dressed model. This is a crisis for Fred and is funny as well. We could have started Act II with Fred back in his suit and used exposition to explain what had happened in the meantime. However, the comedy audience wants to see the resolution of the dilemma, so it is better to start Act II from exactly the same moment as Act I ends.

Endings

Traditionally, comedies have happy endings but there is scope for open endings and even unhappy endings if they can be shown to be absolutely inevitable. In farce, the choice is between the protagonist coming out on top or losing everything. Whichever end is chosen, the audience should believe the opposite is going to happen until the last few lines when the final twist reverses the situation.

Case study: comedy end...

In *Over Exposure*, Fred is convinced that not only will he neve... the money to pay for his campaign, but his wife will have enough ammunition to make his life hell. However, photos of his wife in a compromising situation with the EU bureaucrat save the day and Fred comes out on top.

In *Don't get your Vicars in a Twist* George thinks he has solved all the problems until the final moment when he realizes everything is going to unravel and he is going to lose not only the money but much else as well.

Summary

In this chapter you have learnt:

- to take comedy seriously
- to understand the principles
- to count the laughs.

12

writing for the amateur stage

In this chapter you will learn:
- about amateur drama groups
- how to work in the amateur environment
- how to tailor a script to amateur needs.

The main thing I look for in a new script is: that the writer has got the right balance between writing for themselves and writing for an audience.

Sheila Hannon, creative producer, Show of Strength Theatre Company

Although writing for the amateur theatre follows the same basic rules as any other playwriting, there are some special circumstances to take into account.

How professional?

The first consideration is: how professional is the group you are planning to write for?

Large amateur dramatic groups set a very high standard and could well include professional or semi-professional actors among their number. They may have their own theatre or at least access to a good local venue. They probably produce several plays a year and have a faithful following who are well-informed on drama.

These groups are able to tackle any type of play, so it is not necessary to modify your writing style for them. All you have to do is persuade them to produce your play. If you are sending them an unsolicited script and are nervous about its reception – particularly if you are a member of the group – then take a leaf out of Ronnie Barker's book and write under a pseudonym. That's what Ann did with her first script. You can always come clean when they fall upon it with tears of joy.

Some groups have a policy of putting on plays by local writers as part of their annual programme. Others may run competitions to encourage new writing. In both of these instances it is likely they will want one-act plays so that two or three can be performed during an evening. This is a good way for the new writer to get started.

There will be other smaller amateur groups who may only put on one play a year and have problems finding a script to suit them. There could be many reasons for this. Maybe they can't agree on a script, or they can't afford the script hire fees. They may have a small or large number of actors, or an unusual age range. Perhaps they want a play with a local theme, or their audience will only watch certain types of play and all the popular ones have already been performed. Whatever the reason, this is a good opportunity for the new writer, because you will be able to deliver a script that is tailor-made for their particular requirements.

Actors

Generally speaking, they will fall into one of five categories:

- **Experienced and able to be stretched by a challenging role.** If you are not writing for a specific group it is reasonable to assume that there will be at least two experienced and talented actors in the group.
- **Inexperienced but naturally talented and able to take on a major role.** It is also reasonable to assume there will be at least two more actors with less experience but plenty of talent.
- **Less talented and need a role that is within their capabilities.** There will inevitably be a few members who love being on stage but have little talent, and this is where writing for amateurs is very different from writing for the professional theatre. There is plenty of scope to give these actors something to do with small roles and walk-ons, but this means the cast size will be bigger and the plot will have to accommodate them. You can't ask these actors to do anything that is outside their capabilities.
- **Inexperienced and limited to playing themselves.**
- **The chronic ad-libber.** Ad-libbers are usually jokers who often hate learning lines. They know roughly what they need to say and are happy to wing it from there. Give them a little walk-on part where they cannot do much harm, because there is nothing more frustrating to actors who have learned their lines, and are relying on their cues, have someone on stage making it up as they go along. However, do give them something, because on the night they are often inspired and audiences love ad-libs that are well done.

Script basics

There are a few special considerations involved in producing a script for amateurs. It's best to present a script that is as polished and fully developed as possible. If you offer a rough draft and expect them to work things out in rehearsal you are likely to end up with chaos, everybody offering different ideas and nobody quite sure what they should be doing. For instance, in the script an actor enters *up stage right*, and during rehearsal you decide to change that to *up stage left*. The actor is already struggling to learn their lines, and now they have to remember that one of their entrances has changed. A lot of amateurs will associate their lines with their moves, and so prefer the kind of rehearsals where both are done together. If you constantly make changes, that association is broken and has to be rebuilt.

Just remember that the actors generally come to rehearsal having already done a full day's work. They have to clear their heads of all their real-life concerns and summon up the energy for the rehearsal.

Seating

It may seem strange to put seating at the top of the list of things which need to be taken into account when writing a script for amateur groups but it is very important. Dedicated theatres have raked seating, giving a reasonable view to everybody in the audience, but many amateur groups perform in multi-purpose halls with temporary, non-raked seats. Unless there is raked seating, it is inevitable that those sitting three or more rows back will only see the top half of the actors. So don't have the main action taking place with your characters sitting down – only a few people will see it. It is better to have your characters standing up as much as possible.

Settings

If you are writing for a large cast you must choose a setting that would realistically have a lot of people in it. A hotel foyer is fine, a hotel bedroom won't work. In other words, you will need to choose an open setting, and sacrifice something of the principle of claustrophobia.

Language

Amateur actors are often wonderfully gifted but won't have had any professional training. So check your script extra carefully for anything that might make life difficult for the actors. Keep the lines short, and only write long speeches that are strictly necessary. Try to ensure that the lines follow on logically from what has been said before. Amateur actors sometimes find it hard to learn lines, but they will find it easier to remember the gist of the words, even if they don't remember them exactly, as long as the sequence is coherent. Don't give your actors tongue twisters to say.

Don't repeat lines and don't have lines ending with the same words. Actors pick up their cues from the previous line, and if a line is used more than once the actor may jump back and start all over again or even worse, jump forward and miss out a whole chunk of important plot.

Case study: repeated lines

During rehearsals for *Short, Back and Lies* our leading actress pointed out how many times she had to say 'I'll be with you in a moment Mrs Hetherington'. It was very difficult for her to remember exactly where in the scene she was. Fortunately she coped, but we never made that mistake again.

Performance

Amateur actors often find if difficult to be still on stage. Include some simple business for them to do as well as lines to say. You can also include more stage directions and choreograph the moves on stage, making sure that actors are not left stranded or blocked. In commercial theatre this would be left entirely to the director, but in the amateur world there is often a shortage of people willing to direct. If you present a script that works on stage, an inexperienced director will be grateful, and an experienced director will still find ways to put their own stamp on the piece.

Don't leave inexperienced actors who only have small roles on stage for too long with nothing to do – find a reason to get them off so that they can settle their nerves. Also remember to avoid leaving the stage empty, unless offstage dialogue or sound effects can be heard.

Plot and characters

Start by structuring the plot around between four and six main characters. It is still important to have strong, believable characters and a plot that works on all levels, so you need to do the work on these two aspects. However, if you reach a point where you feel the need for an extra character, instead of trying to work out how to do without them as you would when writing for commercial theatre, you can seize the opportunity to create a small role. Keep the character simple and clearly defined so that the actor finds it easy to play. For very small roles, wait until you have a first draft finished and then look through for opportunities for walk-ons. For instance, if someone phones for a taxi, don't have a character look out of the window and say 'the taxi's here', bring the taxi driver on stage briefly. A play that has been expanded in this way will inevitably lose some of the crispness of a tightly written script for a small cast, so don't overdo it.

If you are writing for a specific group of people, the number of characters in your play will be dictated, to an extent, by the number of people who want to be in it. Also bear in mind that someone may drop out, or get stage fright, or a newcomer may have to be fitted in somehow, so it is useful to create a plot which can add or lose an extra character or two. Crowd scenes can be easily expanded or contracted, and small roles can be shared out among a lot of actors, or doubled up if there is a shortage.

Practicalities

Restrictions

If you have been commissioned, how much freedom will you have to write the play? Has the group just asked for 'something funny' or 'a thriller' and left the rest to you, or have they been more prescriptive and stated exactly what they require? In either case, the group may have unrealistic expectations of what you can do for them.

How many writers?

Will you be writing on your own or with a partner? It can seem a good idea to share the load, particularly if there is a tight deadline and you are a beginner. But will you remain friendly enough with each other to stay the course? (We can argue for days over the construction of a single sentence.) Ground rules will have to be agreed and it is easier if one of you has the final say. Having said this, the upside is that once you have got into a rhythm, the work proceeds much more quickly.

Writing can become even more complicated if it is going to be a group effort. This can happen if the play is going to be part of a pageant or local festivity. The advantage is that brainstorming should throw up plenty of ideas – the disadvantage is that the piece may not have a clear structure. Again, it is easier if one person makes the final choices. There will also need to be a clear understanding of what you are all trying to achieve.

Direction

Once the play is finished, who is going to direct it? In the commercial theatre you can at least assume the director will be a professional, but some amateur groups don't have any members who want to direct. It can also be traumatic handing over to someone else the play you have sweated blood to create. Remember that all directors have their own ideas, so if you don't want someone else muscling in on your masterpiece, you may have to direct it yourself. On the other hand, someone else's input can add a whole new dimension to your work.

Resources

If you are writing for one specific group you can tailor the play exactly to their resources. Even if you are writing for the amateur market generally, you still need to understand that the environment is quite different from the professional theatre. The easiest way to achieve an understanding of this is to join your local amateur group. If you don't want to act, you will be welcomed as part of the backstage crew, or the front-of-house team. The most unpopular job of all is usually the get-out, which is clearing everything away on the day after the last performance, so make yourself available for that if you want to be popular.

Performance space

If you are writing for a specific group then consider the implications of their performance space. Performance in the round, if this is available, can have advantages for amateurs. There is no scope for scenery, and props will have to be kept to a minimum. It is a very intimate way of working and can allow for an interaction between audience and cast. The disadvantages are that some actors might find it both daunting and distracting to have the audience so close to them, and you will need to ensure the action doesn't happen in one direction or only one part of your set.

If there is a stage, what size is it? How many people will it comfortably hold? It is perfectly possible to write a play for a large cast on a small stage, you just mustn't have them all on at the same time. This means always having reasons for plenty of exits and entrances.

Case study: stage size

One of our biggest casts (12) is in *The Tour Starts Here*, which was performed on a tiny temporary stage in a village hall. By setting the play in the corridor that connected the servants' part of a stately home with the grand rooms we could keep cast members constantly on the move.

Scene changes

Will there be curtains? If there aren't any then scene changes will have to be done with the lights out and need to be kept simple. It is perfectly possible to use the same set and create different scenes with the use of props.

Playing to curtains (i.e. black curtains on three sides of the stage) with minimum props, is the simplest choice of all, particularly if you plan to take your play on tour, e.g. around day centres, schools etc.

Case study: simple scene changing

In our play *Freehold and Free* we set the action in a communal hallway and three apartments. The set consisted of the hallway and one basic flat. With each scene change the actors carried on props, such as a rug or a lamp, which indicated which apartment the scene was to take place in.

Backstage

As well as actors you will also need backstage people, and the more complicated the play the more backstage help will be needed. Again, if you are writing for a specific group you will be able to find out what they have available, but there are some general rules for amateur productions.

- **Set.** Don't specify a complicated set, keep things simple. If it works in a village hall then it will work anywhere, and groups with more resources can always embellish the basic set.

- **Lighting.** Again, keep it simple. Don't specify sophisticated lighting effects, although you can indicate places where they would be useful if available.
- **Sound.** Sound effects can make a tremendous difference to a play and can either be pre-recorded or created off-stage when needed. Again keep them simple, and hope that the backstage crew is on the ball. There is nothing worse than a phone ringing after the actor has picked it up or an actor desperately waiting for a door bell to ring.
- **Makeup.** Stage makeup is much lighter these days and most people can cope with doing their own. Beware of writing parts that need special makeup effects such as blood, scars and prosthetics if there is no one available to do them.
- **Props.** Amateur groups can be incredibly inventive with props but most of what you need is going to be scavenged from their own homes and charity shops, so bear this in mind when writing. If a prop is absolutely essential to the plot then make sure it is something reasonably easy to beg, steal or borrow. If you specify trick props, such as a chair that collapses when someone sits on it, you might need to include a note suggesting how it can be done.

Summary

In this chapter you have learnt:

- to get to know the actors
- to fully polish the script before rehearsals start
- to keep things simple
- to add in small roles.

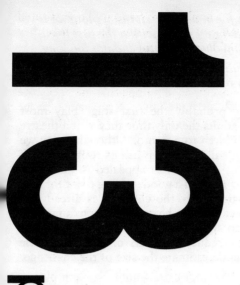

13

pantomimes

In this chapter you will learn:
- about the history of pantomime
- about pantomime conventions
- how to shape a pantomime plot.

The main thing I look for in a new script is: a plot that is largely character based, interests me within the first third, keeps me emotionally involved, truthful and not too long.

Terry Milton, artistic director of the Backwell Playhouse and staff member of the Bristol Old Vic for 35 years

In Britain, pantomime is probably the first stage play most people see, and for many adults the only time they visit a theatre is when they take their children to a panto. Although today we think of it as being traditionally British, it has its roots in Greek drama and in one form or another has appealed to audiences ever since. Panto is fun to write and a good starting point for new writers. The audience, particularly the children, is already on your side, because they have come to be swept away to a magical place and they all want to shout 'he's behind you', join in the community singing and be reduced to tears of laughter by the comedy. However, don't underestimate the size of the challenge.

Professional pantomimes have large casts – unlike straight plays – and big budgets. In order to make this financially viable, pantos are usually put on by companies who re-use the scenery and costumes in different parts of the country over several years. This means the scripts have a long life, and that they generally need a re-write in the autumn of each year to keep them up to date. Panto companies expect their writers to be available to do this.

Plot

Traditionally, pantomimes are based on a small number of well-known fairy stories, the most popular being Cinderella. However there are possibilities in other types of story, especially folk stories such as Robin Hood or fairy stories like Hansel and Gretel.

To sustain a full-length pantomime there has to be a strong simple storyline which incorporates the following elements:

- emotion
- conflict
- twists
- surprises
- black moment
- climax
- resolution.

Endings are easy in pantomimes: the main characters always live happily ever after, the villain is always worsted and the villain's sidekick, if there is one, is always redeemed.

Any of the popular pantomime stories can make a good starting point. The traditional stories aren't copyright – apart from the names of the seven dwarves in Snow White which belong to the Disney Corporation – and you already know the plot.

Plot construction

Generally speaking, pantomimes are written in two acts. After the set-up there is an inciting incident followed by obstacles and finally a resolution which allows the first act to end with a lively finale. The end of the first act is also a good place to have anything messy, such as a custard pie scene, as it gives the crew a chance to clean things up in the interval.

In the second act, there will be a further inciting incident, more obstacles, building to a climax and the final resolution.

Each act will have around six to seven scenes which alternate between front of curtain and full stage. If we take Cinderella for example the story could be broken down as follows:

Scene 1: front of curtain. The Fairy opens the show with a short narration in rhyming couplets.

Scene 2: curtains open to full stage. The set is a village green. Village girls do a song and dance. Enter Cinderella and Buttons. Cinderella wants someone to love.

Scene 3: front of curtain. Enter Prince Charming and Dandini. Prince Charming wants someone to love. They talk about the ball.

Scene 4: curtains open to full stage. The set is Cinderella's kitchen. We meet Cinderella's father the Baron, her Stepmother, who is the Dame, and the Ugly Sisters, who are the baddies. There is plenty of scope for comedy and corny jokes. The invitation to the ball arrives – this is the inciting incident. Cinderella is not invited – this is the first obstacle to her happiness.

Scene 5: front of curtain. The Fairy tells the audience she may be able to help.

Scene 6: front of curtain. Cinderella has been sent out to buy face-packs for the Ugly Sisters. Buttons commiserates with her and they sing a duet.

Scene 7: curtains open to full stage. Same set as Scene 4. The Stepmother and the Ugly Sisters are in a frenzy of activity trying to make themselves look gorgeous. There is more slapstick comedy. They all go off to the ball and Cinderella is left to be comforted by Buttons. Arrival of Fairy Godmother, and transformation of Cinderella – she will go to the ball. This is the resolution to the inciting incident, but with the Fairy's admonition that Cinderella must be home by midnight the seeds of the inciting incident in Act II have been sown. Village girls enter to see how gorgeous she looks, cue for a song from everyone.

CURTAIN AND INTERVAL

Scene 8: curtains open to full stage. The ballroom scene. Clock strikes midnight and Cinderella flees. The striking clock is the inciting incident. The fact that her clothes turn to rags and she has to flee are the obstacles to Cinderella's happiness.

Scene 9: front of curtain. Prince Charming with the glass slipper. He laments the loss of Cinderella, sings a suitable song and resolves to try the slipper on all the ladies in the land.

Scene 10: curtains open to full stage. Same set as Scene 4. The Stepmother and Ugly Sisters discuss the ball and the beautiful stranger who stole the Prince's heart. Enter Buttons bringing news of the Prince and the slipper. More comedy moments as Ugly Sisters try to ensure their feet will fit. This is another obstacle for Cinderella who won't be asked to try the slipper.

Scene 11: front of curtain. Buttons tells the audience he loves Cinderella. He invites children to come up on stage to cheer him up.

Scene 12: curtains open to full stage. Same set as Scene 4. Prince and Dandini arrive to try the slipper on the Ugly Sisters. This is a black moment for Cinderella as the Prince doesn't recognize her and is probably going to marry one of the Ugly Sisters. But there is a twist, the slipper doesn't fit. Finally Buttons, although it is breaking his heart, pushes Cinderella forward. This is the climax – will she be allowed to try the slipper on? She does, it fits, and there is a resolution.

Scene 13: front of curtain. Dandini helps the audience with community singing. It will take him the least time to change for Scene 14 and he will be one of the last on.

Scene 14: curtains open to full stage. A glittery set for the walk-down, with the cast dressed for the wedding of Prince Charming and Cinderella. The principal characters enter followed by

Cinderella and Prince Charming in full wedding regalia. Song from whole company, with perhaps a final verse from the Fairy.

THE END

Pantomime conventions

There are many conventions attached to pantomime (more than most forms of drama), and while it is difficult to break these rules, there is nothing to say they can't be bent a little.

Magic

This is a vital ingredient. Pantomimes are synonymous with the Christmas festivities and should take the audience on a magical ride. There will be at least one character with magical powers, such as the Fairy Godmother or the Genie, and the magic must be integrated into the plot.

Humour

This is a must in pantomimes, and should include slapstick, corny jokes, topical and/or local references and double entendres. It is impossible to make pantomime politically correct, so all the corny old jokes can be given an outing. Custard pies in the face, banana skins on the floor, still raise a laugh – provided the sequence is properly choreographed and performed slickly. Nothing goes down better with an audience than a swipe at the current news. References to popular televisions shows also work well.

Sentiment

There is always a sentimental element in pantomime. You need to wring the audience's heartstrings when the hero or heroine are at their lowest ebb, and the happy ending has to be played at full throttle.

Roles

There has to be a principal boy, a principal girl, a dame, a villain and a good fairy. Supporting roles give each of the principals someone to talk to and minor roles fill the crowd scenes.

Characters tend to be fairly one-dimensional. The villain should be thoroughly wicked and the heroine sweetly feminine. While the main characters are clearly good or evil, the minor characters can be more of a mixture. The villain's sidekick can have a conscience, or one of the basically good characters can succumb to temptation or make a silly mistake.

Cross dressing

No one thinks it's odd that the dame is usually played by a man and the principal boy is played by a woman. Nowadays the principal boy may be played by a male, but it is rare to find the dame played by a woman.

Audience participation

This comes in three forms:

- warning the hero of danger
- joining in community singing
- being invited on stage – usually children.

No panto is complete without the audience being encouraged to shout 'He's behind you' or 'oh no it isn't', or join in the chorus of a song where the words have been written large on a dropdown screen.

Songs

Pantomimes often start with a rousing song and dance routine from the chorus. This sets the scene for the audience and should be as colourful as possible.

They also end with a song, usually with the whole company joining in. In between, songs can move the story forward, tell the audience how the singer is feeling, particularly the principal boy and the principal girl. Unless you are going to write your own, remember that most songs are subject to the rules of copyright, although it is alright to use traditional tunes and folk music.

Dance

In addition to the opening dance, other dance sequences can add a magical factor to the show. Depending on the budget, they can include flying ballets, ice or roller skating or even jitterbugging ·keletons – the main thing is to be imaginative.

Children

Small children performing in costume always add the aaahhh factor. Even when they go wrong the audience will love it. However, it should be born in mind there are regulations regarding children performing on the stage.

Scenery

This plays an important part in pantomime and sets the magical tone. Professional pantomime production is always lavish and technically challenging. In amateur pantomimes, budget and resources will come into it, but with ingenuity and a lot of glitter, it is possible to create scenes with the wow factor.

Front of curtain

These scenes are integral to pantomimes. They not only give time for sets to be changed, but they also allow the comic characters to interact with the audience on a more personal level. There is usually at least one speciality front of curtain scene, where an actor will step out of character briefly to perform conjuring tricks, do acrobatics or show off some other talent – these are only loosely incorporated into the plot, and the audience accepts this.

Animals

Several traditional pantomimes include actors dressed as animals, e.g. Dick Whittington's cat, Mother Goose's goose, Jack and the Beanstalk's cow. These animals can get away with comic or outrageous behaviour that would be frowned on in humans.

Rhyming couplets

These are traditionally reserved for the good fairy or the wicked witch. They can add a whole extra layer to the humour and also move the story on in the form of narration.

Anachronisms

Panto audiences positively relish anachronism (or historical inaccuracies), so that characters wearing eighteenth century clothes and riding around in gilded carriages can also refer to television programmes or pull out a mobile phone.

Walkdown

After the final resolution there is always a walkdown in which all the cast members take a bow. This should start with the members of the chorus, who usually wave to the audience and acknowledge the applause. They then move to the back of the stage and continue to sing (usually a medley of all the songs from the show) while the rest of the cast enter in pairs, one from each side, meet in the middle of the stage and walk to the front while the audience applaud. The final pair is always the two main characters who are going to live happily ever after.

Modern twist

Publishers and producers are looking for pantomimes with a difference so it is worth giving some thought to updating the storyline, while still retaining the traditional conventions.

Case study: a modern twist

With our first pantomime, *Christmas Special With Extra Fried Rice* (written for an amateur group) we looked at what happened after Cinderella and Prince Charming went off to live happily ever after. We took the liberty of assuming they didn't actually get married, but were only engaged, and decided that Prince Charming had lost all his money. We kept all the main characters, and by bringing the action up to date – although we still kept the traditional pantomime clothes – we were able to introduce Chinese takeaways, television game shows and charity shops. A final twist at the end had the audience voting for whether Cinderella should choose Buttons or Prince Charming as her husband.

Summary

In this chapter you have learnt:

- how to structure a pantomime plot
- to have clearly defined good and evil characters
- to always have a happy ending.

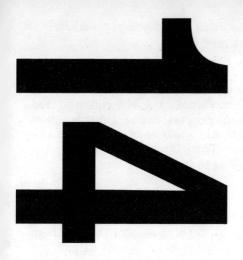

14

musicals

In this chapter you will learn:
- about the history of musical theatre
- how to collaborate on a musical
- about special requirements of musicals.

The most common mistake that new playwrights make is: to impose self-limitations – be bold.

Catherine Johnson, scriptwriter

Like pantomimes, musicals combine songs and dance routines with dramatic content. They should be lively, colourful and move along at a faster pace than normal drama. However, there should also be strong contrasts, so that at times the pace will slow and the mood become sombre.

History

The modern musical, where music, song and plot are all equally important, came into being at the beginning of the twentieth century. Before that, the fashion in America was to pick the most popular arias from an established light opera and write a new book to fit them. To this was added a spectacular production with beautiful showgirls in gorgeous costumes, and a series of spots for comedians. The fashion in England was much the same, except that the music was more likely to be original.

Round about 1915 a move started in America to make the three elements more cohesive, with a properly worked out plot, integrated music, and song lyrics that were intelligent and relevant. One of the pioneers of this movement was the English writer P. G. Wodehouse, who wrote both book and lyrics for various musicals, although he rarely produced both for the same show.

The three elements can all be written by the same person, assuming they have the ability, or by a partnership or by a trio of writers. There is no hard and fast rule, but partnerships seem to be the most successful format.

The book

So, what comes first, the story, the lyrics or the music? There is no one answer – it depends on the librettist, the lyricist and the composer. P. G. Wodehouse preferred to write lyrics to fit the music, whereas W. S. Gilbert liked to write the lyrics and hand them over to Arthur Sullivan to fit to music. But the book is the backbone of a musical, although it is often given the least attention by audience and critics. It is not necessary for the writer to be involved on the music side of things: Catherine Johnson wrote the book for *Mamma Mia!*, where of course the music and lyrics were ready-made in the Abba songs.

Many musicals are based on an existing story, novel or event and these can come from anywhere.

- *Joseph and the Amazing Technicolor Dream Coat* and *Jesus Christ Super Star* come from the Bible.
- *Les Miserables* is based on a Victor Hugo story of the same name.
- *Evita* is based on political events in Argentina.

Before you start work, ask yourself why the story needs to be told as a musical – what will the music add to the story? If the answer is 'nothing' then you are probably wasting your time.

Top tip

Try watching two films, *The Philadelphia Story* and *High Society*. Since they are both taken from the same play (*The Philadelphia Story* by Frederick Knott) you will be able to see how the music changes the experience. Alternatively, watch the film of George Bernard Shaw's *Pygmalion* and the film of *My Fair Lady*, the musical version.

The plot

Most musicals have two acts. As in straight drama, Act I should set up the conflicts to come in Act II. The principles of dramatic construction still apply and the plot must be driven by conflict in a series of dramatic arcs that raise the stakes each time, leading to a crisis followed by a climax.

A musical needs a strong simple plot with believable and well contrasted characters. Because the music takes up around half the show, the storyline is usually briefer than a stage play (see *Into the Woods* by Stephen Sondheim for an exception to this rule). The dialogue should flow seamlessly into the music. The music heightens and enlarges the emotional content of the book, which is why the basic plot needs to be more straightforward than in a straight play. However, the principles of parallelism still apply, so that the what-happens-next part of the plot provides the vehicle for the emotional part of the plot. Keep subplots to a minimum, and aim for an elegant construction where the subplot echoes the main plot.

Case study: parallel plots in a musical

In *Guys and Dolls* by Loesser, Swerling and Burrows, the what-happens-next plot concerns the efforts of Nathan Detroit to raise enough money to pay the rent on the venue for his illegal gambling activities. He bets gambler Sky Masterton that he'll never get Sister Sarah Brown to fly to Cuba for a date with him – he's sure Sky will lose the bet and have to pay him the money he needs. The emotional plot takes off when Sky woos Sarah with the cold-blooded intention of winning the bet. They fall in love, and have to find a way of reconciling their completely different philosophies and lifestyles. Nathan has his own emotional plot in the story of his relationship with nightclub singer Miss Adelaide, which forms a subplot and counterpoint to the main romantic story.

Characters

Musicals have much larger casts than other types of drama, apart from pantomimes, and it is tempting to use extra characters to move the plot forward, but this is not a good idea. The plot should be so tightly drawn that every character seems essential. Also it is not good enough to design a plot around a few characters and then add on a random chorus – they must be there for a reason. Generally there are between four and six principal characters and various secondary characters who step out of the chorus when needed. This movement helps integrate the chorus into the action of the musical.

Musical performers are a special breed, who can usually act, sing and dance, so it is no longer necessary to write speciality roles for a performer with just one type of ability.

The music

The plot should indicate the places where the music will occur. It must be an intrinsic part of the story and not songs which have been slotted in. It should move the plot along and reveal character in the same way as dialogue, with a strong emphasis on emotional content. This means that songs are placed at moments of heightened emotion, and often at the end of a scene.

The story, the singing and the choreography should all combine in a seamless flow. Avoid setting up a song by having a character suggest it – this isn't necessary, the audience knows they have come to see a musical after all. The show should open with a strong number from the chorus and the final song should be, literally, a show stopper.

The lyrics

If you have never written lyrics before, start by reading the lyrics of songs that you know well. They will look quite different on the page – they won't make much sense, and they often don't even seem to work as poetry, so you need to get used to this. Then try writing new lyrics for a tune you know well, before moving on to the challenge of writing lyrics for original music.

It is worth bearing in mind that you do not always need a composer. Like *Mama Mia!,* it is possible to base a musical on existing music rather than original compositions. You will need permission from the owners of the copyright, but there is a wealth of good music out there which could form the basis of a musical.

Placing your work

From a writer's point of view, musicals are probably the most difficult field to break into because of the astronomical costs involved in staging a production. London theatres are not going to take a chance on a new playwright unless they come up with something outstanding. There may be more opportunities in the world of amateur light opera and musical groups where shows such as *Grease* and *The Little Shop of Horrors* are always popular. School drama groups are often very keen on musicals and may consider a new work if it is on a relevant subject.

Summary

In this chapter you have learnt:

- about collaboration when writing a musical
- about sources for plots
- how to integrate the music into the plot.

15

radio drama

In this chapter you will learn:
- about special requirements for radio
- about working with sound
- about dialogue in radio drama.

The main thing I look for in a new radio drama script is: that the dramatist is thinking in terms of radio as a medium, rather than visually for the stage or screen. Using sounds to move us between location, to move the story on. Not that sounds aren't visual, they are: it's just a different way of imagining the pictures – subtly evoking them in our mind's eye. In this way there's enormous potential for interior and intimate thought, which can contrast with the public face the character presents to the world.

Mark Smalley, BBC Radio 4 drama producer

Radio offers the writer unlimited scope for writing a play about:

- absolutely anything
- set absolutely anywhere
- featuring absolutely anyone or anything.

It is an intimate form of storytelling which allows the listener to use their imagination and be gripped by what they are hearing. It is possible to conjure up in the listeners' minds scenarios ranging from the most surreal science fiction – such as Douglas Adams' *Hitchhikers Guide to the Galaxy* – to the most profound depiction of the human condition.

Case study: realism in radio

The American radio adaptation of H. G. Wells' *The War of the Worlds* on Hallowe'en night 1938, was so convincingly realistic that it caused a panic when listeners really believed that New Jersey was being invaded by Martians.

Top tip

Before you try to write for radio, listen to a selection of radio plays and analyse how sound alone is used to create the drama. Pay particular attention to the length of the drama, which is the one unchangeable factor. It dictates, to a certain extent, the scale and scope of the narrative. Also, listen at different times of the day to see how the output varies.

Practicalities

Like any other drama, radio plays need to follow the basic rules of character, dialogue and construction. But there is one important difference which the writer must take into account – the only information the listener receives is via their ears. All the images the writer wishes to create in the listener's mind comes from what is heard. Although information about the play's setting may be given by the continuity announcer or as part of the very start of the play, there is no guarantee that the listener will have switched on at that point, so it is down to the writer to ensure that all this information is subtly included in the body of the writing.

Creating sound pictures

We all know that the pictures are better on radio. This is because the listener, assisted by the writer, will create the pictures in their imagination. Give your listeners the right raw material and they will build mental images that surpass any screen extravaganza or theatrical effect. But never remind them that they can't see the action, for example by revealing late in a play that a character has a beard. This can be annoying if it contradicts a picture that the listener has been building.

There are five ways the listener receives the information they need to build the picture:

- dialogue
- sound effects
- background atmosphere
- music
- silence.

It isn't necessary to use all five elements in every scene or even in every play, but it is the way that they are woven together which creates a sound picture in the listener's mind.

Dialogue

Generally speaking, radio plays are shorter than stage plays, so it is even more essential that every piece of dialogue contributes something. Check each line and if it is not essential take it out.

In a radio play, in addition to moving the story forward – revealing a character's emotional state and showing the relationship between characters – the dialogue also has to give information which in a stage play would be visually obvious. It has to indicate where the action is taking place and what is actually happening. However, this needs to be slotted in carefully.

 Case study: using the dialogue to indicate location

Character A arrives at character B's house.

CHARACTER B: Come into the kitchen for a cup of coffee.

This tells the listener that the characters are going into the kitchen and why – but it's a bit clunky and only gives one piece of information. A small re-write improves this no end:

CHARACTER B: Coffee?

CHARACTER A: I see you went ahead and had a new kitchen then.

Now we not only learn where they are, we also learn that B has conventional good manners and A is rather nosey.

Sound effects

These can have several useful roles:

- Sounds created by what a character is doing such as pouring milk or driving a car.
- Sounds which characters respond to such as telephones and door bells.
- Background noises such as the crackling of a log fire or the hooting of an owl. Once the scene is established these sounds fade under the dialogue.
- Informing the listener about when and where the action is happening, such as the muffled sound of horses' hooves conjuring up a hansom cab in Victorian London, or radiophonics to create a moonscape.
- Cranking up emotional atmosphere, such as a creaking door or footsteps on the stairs to create fear.
- Inducing laughter such as when the sound of a crashing car, falling masonry and tinkling glass is followed by the character saying: 'No, I'm fine, I just tripped over the cat'.

Background atmosphere

Technically, sound engineers can create a different feel for outdoor or indoor scenes, and outdoor scenes in different types of weather and indoor scenes in small or large spaces.

Also, increasingly, plays are made on location, and embrace the soundscape they are set in. This is the basic environment that the writer works with and builds on.

Music

This can be used to enhance a mood or divide scenes. Not all plays require music, others may revolve round it.

Silence

Although it may seem odd to use silence in a medium which relies on sound, dramatic pauses are just as important on radio as in other forms of drama.

However, the listener won't appreciate a silence if they don't understand what is going on. There are some important rules to bear in mind:

- Establish early in the scene who is present.
- Don't have characters who don't say anything unless this is intentional.
- If there is nothing for a character to contribute to the scene, make sure the listener knows they have left the scene.
- If they are keeping quiet for a dramatic reason, make sure the listener knows this.
- If another character enters the scene, make sure the listener is given this information; don't have the character suddenly join in a conversation as if out of nowhere, unless of course they have been sneaking up and make the other characters jump.
- If a character needs to overhear something, make sure the listener knows they are there eavesdropping.

This doesn't mean that every character has to be introduced to the listener. For example, if a character has left the scene, but if the audience knows that they will be returning, it doesn't come as a shock when they speak. A few footsteps or a door opening will be the cue to the listeners that the character has returned.

Characters' voices

It can be confusing to the listener if you have too many characters. The listener has to identify the character from their voice and speech mannerisms, so don't introduce too many in one go.

- **Voice.** Try to avoid everyone speaking with exactly the same accent, as this makes it hard for the listener to tell them apart. Although in real life we don't tend to keep repeating a person's name, on radio it is important because this is another clue as to which character is being addressed.

  Remember that the actors can't use action, facial expression or body language to convey nuances of meaning, to emphasize meaning or to reveal underlying contradictions – all of this has to be in the dialogue.

- **Inner voices.** Unlike most drama, radio offers the listener the chance to hear what a character is thinking as well as saying, rather like a novel. It may be they are one and the same thing – but it adds another layer if they are directly opposite. This can be used to create conflict, or intrigue – and can the listener believe the inner voice?

  The inner voice can also be used for exposition, but remember that background information should be given as part of the plot, or should arise out of the character's emotional and/or physical state. Generally, we only hear one inner voice and that is usually the protagonist.

- **Narrator.** Using a narrator is a device rarely employed nowadays for setting the scene, explaining what has gone before, describing the characters, driving the plot forward and/or clarifying the resolution. However, if used the narrator should be an essential part of the plot and not someone grafted on as an easy way to enlighten listeners. In some plays the inner voice of the protagonist acts as a narrator. In other plays the narrator can be a character in their own right

- **Monologues.** Radio lends itself to monologues, but these need to be extremely well written. If the listener is only going to hear one voice then it needs to be a good one, telling a gripping story. There is a difference between a monologue and a short story, in that a monologue is character based, and the speaker needs to be on a journey within the timeframe of the monologue.

Settings

In radio the writer is spoilt for choice. Your setting can encompass the universe, a farmhouse kitchen or the mind of an animal. But no matter how surreal your setting, it is important to make it authentic. If you don't believe it is possible to hold an identity parade in the hold of a spaceship on its way to Orion

5,000 years into the future, then neither will your listener. Whatever world you create for your play, you need to understand its internal rules and stick to them rigorously.

Plots

It is easy for listeners to turn off a radio play and therefore it is important to have a strong storyline that draws them in from the first word or sound effect and that keeps them hooked. Listeners make a decision about whether to switch off or carry on listening within the first few minutes, so the writer of radio drama does not have the luxury enjoyed by the stage dramatist of having a captive audience – he or she has to sweep them into the story immediately and then hold them. Radio has some distinct advantages when it comes to plot.

- **Subplots.** As it is easy to cut from one subplot to another, radio drama offers more scope for multi-stranded stories than other forms of drama.
- **Scenes.** Radio plays can be set in one location, but they are more interesting if divided into scenes. Unlike stage plays, radio allows the writer to cut to other people, other places and other times. As long as you take your listener with you, it is possible to include scenes lasting only seconds, but which add colour and drama to the plot.
- **Show don't tell.** This still applies, but not in a visual sense – in other words, characters must reveal themselves, and the plot must unfold, through dramatic events rather than reported descriptions. Radio has the advantage of allowing the listener to hear something happening rather than have it described verbally.

Genres

Radio offers the writer a greater range of genre than stage or television because there are fewer budget constrictions and no visual constraints. Basically this means that radio can use novelistic genres such as historical fiction, or multi-generation family sagas. Settings can move from country to country, there are no restrictions on crowd scenes, and no worries about persuading actors to age-up.

The market for radio drama

Every week around a dozen new plays of varying length and genre are broadcast by the BBC. This means that the playwright can immerse themselves in the medium without having to go out of the door – giving the opportunity to study what makes a good play and also what makes a bad play. Even if you miss a play on the radio it is now possible to listen to it on your computer via the Internet. The second advantage is that there is a steady market for good radio drama.

At the time of writing, Radio 4 broadcasts five 15-minute plays in Woman's Hour; several 30-minute plays or series, usually comedy, at 11:30; five 45-minute afternoon plays and one 60-minute play on Friday evenings; one 60-minute play on Saturday afternoon. Radio 3 has a 90-minute play on Sundays and the World Service broadcasts a 60-minute play also on Sundays. BBC 7 offers some opportunity for new writing, but much of its content is repeats of old material. However, BBC drama commissioners are more willing to be experimental with BBC 7, so it can offer a good way in for new writers.

A large proportion of BBC drama is commissioned and produced in-house, but a percentage of plays have to come from independent producers. The independents as a whole are less likely to take a risk with a new writer than the BBC.

Placing a radio play

At the time of writing, the BBC Writersroom handles unsolicited scripts. They will only look at completed scripts and are not interested in outlines or proposals. The only exception is with 30-minute series when the advice is to send one fully-written episode, not necessarily the first, and then outlines for the rest of the episodes, with character descriptions and how the series will work. They do not accept e-mail submissions. Do not send your only copy.

It is possible to send a play directly to a BBC producer, but there is no guarantee they will have time to read it, whereas all scripts that go via the Writersroom will be read. (See Taking It Further for details.)

Summary

In this chapter you have learnt:

- to work with sound alone
- to create characters based on voice
- about the market for radio plays.

16

writing for television

In this chapter you will learn:

- about television drama
- how to structure a script for television
- about technical matters.

The main thing I look for in a new script is: the irresistible motivation to turn the page.

John Bruce, television drama director

Most of us watch more television drama than anything else and there is plenty of variety. Soaps, sitcoms and detective stories can all be classed as drama, as well as one-off plays, continuing series like *Casualty* and *Heartbeat*, and drama serials like *Bleak House*.

The fact that it is beamed into our homes makes it easier to study, and if you want to write for television it will be necessary to dissect every piece of drama you watch rather than just enjoying it on a superficial level. This will probably spoil your enjoyment of some programmes when you see the flaws in the writing and production – but it is a good learning experience.

You will also need to study the various genres and take note of their particular requirements such as content and running times and whether they are before or after the nine o'clock watershed.

At the time of writing:

- BBC single dramas are 90 minutes long
- drama series are 30 or 50 minutes per episode
- drama serials are 60 minutes an episode
- soaps and sitcoms are 30 minutes per episode
- occasionally the BBC transmits 30-minute self-contained plays, but these are generally commissioned.

Dramatic construction

The same basic rules apply whether you are writing a 30-minute sitcom or a 90-minute self-contained drama. They will need conflict to power the plot, a crisis, a climax and a resolution. But remember, television is a visual medium and you will need to see the plot in visual terms from the beginning (see Storyboarding on page 171). It is vitally important to keep in mind the rule 'show don't tell'.

Characters

Television is a more personal medium than stage. The cameras beam us right into the heart of the action. We get up close and personal with the characters. Strong characterization is therefore essential.

As television allows us to see the characters in many different situations it is even more essential for the writer to know their characters intimately and how they will react in any circumstance. Television can be unforgiving to writers who don't create well-rounded characters and show them, warts and all. But remember, although television is a visual medium, dialogue still plays an important part and fulfils the same basic functions as in any drama.

Trigger, exposition and foreshadowing

Like radio, the viewer can switch off if the play doesn't grab their interest from the word go – so start the drama as near to the trigger point as possible. This immediately pulls the viewer into the action.

Exposition is easier on television. The saying 'a picture paints a thousand words' springs to mind here because, unlike stage and radio, dialogue is not always needed to explain the back-story – a brief visual shot of something which happened previously can set the scene. Sometimes the exposition is done in a series of flashbacks. However you choose to do it, the exposition must be done subtly and remember to only give enough information for the audience to understand what is going on.

Case study: exposition

When a short film of our stage play *Living Doll* was made, an opening shot of Kevin's chaotic living room established that he was a messy slob, and also showed an urn of ashes on the mantelpiece. We cut quite a lot of the play's opening dialogue, and instead Kevin just patted the urn and said 'Morning Mum' to tell the audience that she had died.

Depending on the type of drama, there will be occasions when the writer wants the viewer to know more than some of the characters do. This technique is often used in thrillers when the audience are informed from the beginning who the murderer is and their interest is held by how the police solve the crime.

As with exposition, television gives the writer the opportunity to foreshadow by using visual scenes which are set in the future, as well as through dialogue.

Subplots

Like radio there is more opportunity for subplots – even a 30-minute soap will have one or two subplots. Apart from adding interest and texture to your script, they allow you to cut away from one plot line to another. In this case every scene must have a specific part to play in the drama – if it doesn't, then dump it. Some scenes might be as short as a few seconds, others will be longer, but it is rare to find a really long scene.

Scenes

Apart from traditional sitcoms, which are studio based and filmed in front of an audience, television drama generally includes both interior and exterior scenes.

Scenes also have an additional role in television drama – sometimes they take over the functions of dialogue. We have already said that a non-verbal scene can be used for exposition and foreshadowing, but they can also be used to move the plot forward, reveal information, or reveal something about a character in the same way that dialogue does in a stage play. In addition, in comedies, they can also create a laugh. However, because the viewers are used to the way television drama works it isn't necessary to spell everything out. For example, we don't need to see every movement a person makes to get from A to B. If we see a man driving down the road looking for a house and the next shot is the interior of the house and the doorbell is ringing we aren't surprised to see the man on the doorstep. This is called a jump-cut, and it keeps the action moving.

Cut to

It is usual to indicate the end of a scene with the words 'Cut to'. This technique allows you to progress the main plot and several subplots at the same time, by cutting from one to the other. Sometimes there is an obvious link between the main plot and the various subplots, but it heightens the viewers' interest if the subplots seem to be completely unrelated. Of course, the viewers know that all the strands will come together by the end of the drama but it is how the writer does this that keeps them watching. Clearly it makes sense to cut away from a scene at a moment of crisis and return to it for the climax and resolution.

Cutting to another scene also gives the opportunity of moving the plot forward in time and avoiding unnecessary scenes. If the protagonist's home has been trashed we don't need to see them clearing up the mess or dealing with the police. Cutting to another subplot not only avoids unwanted footage and characters, but moves another part of the story forward. The technique can be used to ratchet up the tension, such as cutting to another scene just when a piece of vital information is about to be revealed.

Sets

When television drama first started in the late 1940s and early 1950s, the directors came from theatrical backgrounds and the sets had three walls exactly like a stage set. Everything went out live so several cameras were used, all linked to an editing control panel where the vision mixer cut all the shots together. This gave a theatrical feel to the dramas.

Today one of the biggest pitfalls to avoid is writing television drama which looks stagey. A writer who has been used to writing for the narrow confines of a stage may find it hard to stretch out and take full advantage of the medium. But plays written with the stage in mind do not look good on television – just adding a couple of exterior shots to a stage play won't work.

Nowadays, constructed sets in a studio are rarely used except for sitcoms and soaps – it is cheaper to pay a location fee. For example the long-running series *Holby City* and *Casualty* use a converted former hospital. However, even if the interior scenes take place on a set built for the purpose, any resemblance to a stage ends there because of the way it is used. A good example is *The Royle Family*, which is often filmed with most of the characters sitting down in a row watching television, but the use of different camera angles, close-ups and the occasional shot of an adjoining room dispel any notion in the viewers' mind that they are watching a stage play.

Understanding the camera

The biggest difference between television and stage or radio is the camera – and this must be taken into account when writing a television drama. Everything that the viewer sees comes via the camera, and it is how the camera is used which differentiates television drama from other forms.

How much camera direction should the writer include in their script? Nowadays, the convention is for very little shot description or camera direction – a possible exception being when a close-up is absolutely needed to tell the story. However, a good director with whom you have built a relationship will always involve the writer or at least have a meeting to discuss the script. Having said that, even though it could be down to the director to decide on the camera shots, it is important for the writer to understand what can and can't be done.

The fourth wall

Because most dramas are filmed on location, the set now has a fourth wall, which allows shots to be taken from various angles – even reverse ones. Because the dramas never go out live, only one or possibly two cameras are used, and it is then down to the editor to pull the shots together and create the final version.

Hand-held cameras and moving cameras

Hand-held cameras are lightweight, easily portable and give the viewers the feeling that they are right in the centre of the action.

Moving cameras are able to follow characters from one room to the next or along a road and thus are able to extend a scene rather than having to cut to another one. It pulls the viewers into the action and cranks up the drama. For example, the American drama series *West Wing* uses quite long sequences where the major characters stride through the offices and corridors in the White House, while engaging in conversations, reading documents, drinking coffee and anything else the writers can come up with. While not suggesting the writer adopts this trademark style of drama in its entirety, use of this technique makes television drama dynamic in a way that cannot be matched on stage.

Camera angles and close-ups

Cameras can be angled away from one character to focus on another. This can show their reaction to what the first character is either saying or doing. Or it can show that they are oblivious to the first character and their reaction is to something entirely different. Whether the viewer sees what they are reacting to depends on whether the writer is ready to reveal it or not.

Close-ups make television drama an intimate medium. They can be used by the writer to enhance a dramatic moment such as focusing the grief shown by a character on learning a loved one has died. They can also be used as visual exposition or foreshadowing.

Cameras also allow the writer to stipulate which point of view they want. For example, the viewer can see an overall view or the view as seen by one of the characters.

Plotting

Storyboarding

Although the same rules of drama apply, such as set-up, trigger and payoff, television is a visual medium and the viewers are able see what is happening, so they don't need to be told. One way of writing visually for television is to use storyboarding. This is a technique used in screenwriting, but it can be a useful tool when preparing the first draft of a television script.

Like a cartoon strip, the play is divided into short scenes, but rather than drawing a picture, write in everything you want each scene to do. For example in our television sitcom *Dandelion and Burdock* the opening scene is a burial. We needed to see the reactions of all the mourners as well as the Minister taking the service so we wrote a list of all the things we wanted the characters to be seen to be doing.

A group of people surround an open grave as a vicar conducts the service.

Among them we see Saville, who is wearing a camel overcoat, surreptitiously trying to make a phone call on his mobile.

Hermione, who is wearing a waxed jacket and jodhpurs, stamping her feet with cold and constantly glancing at her watch.

Joyce, who is dressed in black, sobbing into her handkerchief.

Aunty, who is wearing an old fur coat, moving among the mourners and picking their pockets.

The Minister comes to the end of the service and Hermione places a butler's tray on the coffin and hurries back to a line of waiting cars. Saville follows her. Joyce throws a rose onto the coffin then turns away weeping and stumbles after them. Aunty shakes hands with the Minister, he looks pleased.

Aunty gets in the car next to Hermione looking pleased. We look back at the Minister who suddenly realizes he is no longer wearing his surplice. He looks for his watch, from his reaction we know that it has disappeared.

In the above scene there is really no need for dialogue. But if it is necessary, it can be put in once all the scenes have been storyboarded in the same way.

Top tip

Remember, as the writer it is unlikely you will have any say in the editing process and it maybe that one or more of your lines or even scenes will have to be sacrificed. There is usually a good reason for this, perhaps because of time constraints or because the editor was trying to create a certain balance.

Summary

In this chapter you have learnt:

- to keep it dynamic
- to keep it visual
- to avoid staginess.

section

three

17

script practicalities

In this chapter you will learn:
- about theatricality
- how to tailor your script to the stage.

The most common mistake that new playwrights make is:
imparting information to an audience through characters
telling other characters what they already know.

John Bruce, television drama director

Theatricality

One of the most common reasons for a play being rejected is 'it's not theatrical'. This implies that there is nothing much wrong with the plot and the characters, but that the story is not told in a way that lends itself to the stage. It can mean that the writer hasn't paid sufficient attention to technical matters, and so the script demands lighting or scenery that is either impossible or wildly expensive. However, the most likely meaning is that the play is actually a television script, not a stage play. We are all saturated with television from an early age, and inevitably when we first start to think about writing a drama we tend to think in television terms. This isn't a crime; it's just a habit that has to be broken by anyone who wants to write for the stage.

Simple mistakes immediately tell a script reader that the play has come from a novice and reveal a television bias, for instance:

- assuming that an actor's face can be seen in close-up
- assuming that somehow the audience can pan across the stage like a camera
- too many changes of location
- swift cutting from scene to scene.

Audiences experience theatre in quite a different way from television. Very few people now sit down to watch television in a darkened room with no distractions. Instead, we watch and live our lives at the same time. Conversations continue, meals are eaten and the television carries on talking to itself in the corner of the room. On the other hand, those who go to the theatre have put their life on hold for an evening. They sit in the dark and give their full attention to the performance. This means that they expect more of the experience, but also that they bring more to it.

There are similarities with the experience of cinema going, but watching too many films will still lead a writer into mistakes of scale and dramatic development. Theatre is more intimate than film, and film scripts are nothing like play scripts as a result.

Obscenity, sex and blasphemy

There is no official censorship in the United Kingdom, but inevitably some subjects are considered more challenging than others. Theatre producers and creative directors make their own decisions about what is acceptable on stage, and have to hope that audiences agree with them. What is acceptable in a small venue at the Edinburgh Fringe may be completely unacceptable in mainstream commercial theatre.

The important thing from the writer's point of view is to write the play you passionately believe in without censoring yourself and then decide whether it has a chance of being produced. If you feel that your subject is too difficult to be approached directly, then consider using a metaphor to tell your story.

It goes without saying that swearing, nudity and so on should never be put into a play just to make it more shocking – there must always be a good reason.

Length and timing

The length of a drama can be anything from the few minutes of a sketch to an entire evening – or even (but rarely) several evenings, such as the Royal Shakespeare Company's production of *Nicholas Nickleby*, or Alan Ayckbourn's play *Intimate Exchanges* which offers eight major variations – although usually only two or three are staged at a time. Most dramas fall between these extremes.

The first decision to make is whether your play be:

- **One act.** A one-act play should run for between 30 and 45 minutes, so that two or three of them will provide an evening's entertainment. Occasionally, competitions call for shorter one-act plays. Generally speaking, the professional stage prefers full length while amateur groups are happy to take on one-acts. Most amateur drama festivals and many writing competitions are based on one-act plays, so that there is a constant demand for them.

or

- **Full length.** If full length, your play will need to be in at least two acts. While the writer may feel that the dramatic construction of the play should dictate the number of acts, they still need to take into account the requirements of the professional stage, which is mainly geared towards two acts. Most modern plays tend to have two acts. This gives one interval and works well in the commercial theatre.

The length of your play will depend on the type of drama, whether you have enough material to sustain a full length play, and where you hope to place it.

Timing a piece can be difficult, and performances will tend to vary because of the effect of different audiences – actors are very sensitive to audience reactions. To get a rough idea, read your play aloud and time yourself. Allow only a few seconds for each stage direction – the business of a play generally takes very little time. As a very rough guide, an A4 page of script, properly laid out, takes about a minute to perform.

Cast size

Mainstream theatre economics dictate that modern serious plays have small casts, which in turn means that there are not very many secondary characters and certainly no crowd scenes.

If you are writing for a small touring company there is often a requirement for a small part for the Assistant Stage Manager, or ASM. The job is usually done by a young actor at the start of their career and while they are needed off-stage for most of the performance they can also play a small role. Also very small roles can be doubled up, with one actor playing two or more parts.

Less commercial forms of theatre are more flexible and may accommodate a greater number of characters. Amateur groups often want small roles for new or less confident members of the company, and the same is true of school productions, pageants and community theatre. On some drama courses the students have to give a performance that is adjudicated, and scripts with larger casts are needed for these.

Even in the professional theatre some genres, such as pantomime, musicals and some forms of comedy, have large casts with many secondary and minor characters. These characters can be a joy to write, because they can be much more extreme than the central characters. Think of Prince Charming and Cinderella – nice enough, and their story gives the plot its backbone, but we are much more entertained by the outrageous Ugly Sisters, the feeble Baron and the evil Baroness.

Openings

The usual convention is for plays to open onto an empty stage. As with most conventions, it can be disregarded, but you need to be aware that both actors and audience will find it unsettling. The first few minutes of a play have a difficult task. The audience will not yet be fully focused on the play – they will be settling into their seats, turning off their phones, opening their sweets. You haven't got them yet. However, you do need to catch their attention, and quickly. They have paid for their tickets and they want to be entertained, and they won't wait too long for you to get on with it.

Whatever you do in the opening seconds, don't convey any important information. If the audience misses the moment when the brigadier opens the letter from a secret admirer, they may never catch up with what is going on.

Top tip

One simple technique is to write something without dialogue, something funny or arresting – a character enters breathless, and struggles to speak, or clutches their chest, staggers and collapses. The actor can time this business until they feel that the audience has settled – then the play can proceed. Another idea is to use shock or surprise to gain attention – a gunshot rings out, or a scream. Another useful tool is to have minor characters come on stage first to set up the entrance of the major characters.

Entrances and exits

As these play such an important part in the plot it is essential to get them right. All credibility will be lost with the audience if you get it wrong.

We once spent the entire interval of a two-act play wondering why a character who had exited to the kitchen suddenly re-appeared via the front door. The answer could only be that it suited the writer, but the result was we were unable to pay much attention to the rest of the play.

Unless you have given the audience the information that it is possible for anyone going out of one entrance to come back in another one, characters should always come back in the same way as they went out. To have a character exit to a room from which, as far as the audience knows, there is no other way out, and then for that character to enter from a completely different place, is cheating your audience – and they may not forgive you. Not everyone will spot what you've done, but many audience members will come away with a vague feeling of something not being right. So, if a character exits to the kitchen and returns via the front door, this must be explained, but if they return from the kitchen, nothing needs to be said.

As has been said in Chapter 05, the entrance of a new character or the reappearance of an existing one can have a transforming effect on the dynamics of a scene. This can be further heightened by how the character enters:

- Someone climbing in through a window creates a different impression to someone coming through a door.
- A character that can be seen by the audience through a window before they make their entrance can heighten anticipation.

There was a convention that major characters always entered from up centre to give the most impact. However, these decisions mainly lie with the director and could also be influenced by the set design.

Case study: entrances

In *Over Exposure*, the main character is described as being as cool as a cucumber and then arrives in a state of total panic. As a result the audience is immediately intrigued and amused.

There will be times when the writer desperately needs a character to be off stage for some reason. But remember, exits should be plausible parts of the plot:

- Some exits will be precipitated by something which happens on stage and may be preceded by some sort of remark, such as 'I'll go and make some tea'.
- Other exits will be caused because of something that happens off stage – a doorbell rings for instance. In this case, when the character returns, something needs to be said about it. Remember that everything in a play happens for a reason.
- If a character has been gone for some time and then returns, there should be some indication either visually or verbally as to what they have been doing while they were gone.

- Exits and entrances can also be used to indicate character traits. If one character says 'Make some tea, there's a love', and the other character exits silently, we have learnt something – probably that they are a subservient type, willing to do another's bidding.

On a practical level the writer will need to take into account the logistics of exiting:

- When a character has to exit, try to ensure that their last speech is made near that exit. This will save them walking right across the stage and spoiling the moment.
- Always check that characters who have left the stage are not likely to bump into each other in the imagined off stage world – if one character leaves by the front door and seconds later another enters the same way, then the audience will assume they will have met in the hall and seen each other. If you don't want them to see each other, then give them different exit and entrance points.
- If a character has to exit because they have to undergo some kind of transformation, such as change their costume or turn into a vampire, do ensure the script gives them time to achieve this before they have to come back on.

To summarize, you must make sure that there is a reason for every exit, and for every entrance – go through the script, and write the reason in. Then decide how much the audience needs to know about the reason in each case. It won't be necessary to explain every single action – that would make for a very boring play – but you need to know the reasons.

Top tip

One easy way to check entrances and exits is to make a model stage from a cardboard box and use toy plastic figures or spice jars for the characters. Label them so you can't get confused and go through the script moving your characters on and off stage.

Summary

In this chapter you have learnt:

- to be theatrical
- to give an audience time to settle
- to check entrances and exits.

18

staging practicalities

In this chapter you will learn:
- about settings and scene changes
- about ending acts
- about working with the cast and crew.

> *The most common mistake that new playwrights make is: to include too much production detail and too many stage directions – leave it to the director to interpret in an individual way.*
>
> **Terry Milton, artistic director of the Backwell Playhouse and staff member of the Bristol Old Vic for 35 years**

Performance spaces

The theatre is a physical medium that exists in space and in real time. If you want your script to be performed rather than languishing in a drawer at home, you need to give some consideration to the practicalities of staging.

Performances take place in anything from a village hall through to the biggest and best equipped theatres in the West End or on Broadway.

The three main categories of dedicated theatre are:

- the proscenium arch
- theatre in the round
- the projecting or apron stage.

Settings

Although it is possible to create virtually any setting on stage, budget will inevitably be the dominant factor. So it is probably better not to set your play behind a waterfall which demands a Niagara-type flow throughout the production. The simpler the setting, the more the likelihood the play will be produced, and playing to curtains (i.e. no scenery) with the minimum amount of props, could make all the difference between a company being able to afford a production or not.

Audience expectation is key here. No one buying a ticket for a pub theatre performance expects spectacular staging, while someone going to a West End musical would be rightly disappointed with a low-budget production.

Scene changes

It used to be the convention that scene changes had to be carried out without the audience being aware of them, but modern audiences are used to a wide variety of approaches to scene changing.

Scenes can be changed:

- behind the curtains
- with the lights down and the stage in darkness
- in front of the audience with the clever use of technology
- in front of the audience with no attempt to disguise the change.

A scene can be changed by using the same basic set, but altering it with different props or a change in the lights.

Ending acts

Each act of a play should end with an unresolved crisis, but as far as practical staging is concerned some things are easier at the end of an act. Any kind of chaos on stage – such as the litter from a pantomime fight or overturned furniture – can be quietly removed during the interval. If the actors in a pantomime are covered in custard pies then they can use the interval to clean it off.

Also, if you are left with a dead body at the end of Act I it is easier to clear everything away during the interval rather than having the actors struggle off stage with a corpse. This will also dispense with the need for extra characters, such as police, doctors, ambulance men, who in real life would be involved in a sudden death. It is then possible to start Act II, minutes, hours or days later, and use exposition to explain to the audience what happened while they were away. This is one of the few situations in which the writer can break the 'show don't tell' rule.

Top tip

It is a stage convention that in a comedy a corpse can be left on stage, but in every other type of play it is normal to remove it.

Actors, directors and others

All forms of drama are ultimately group activities. In the modern theatre the writer generally has very little involvement in performance, and the director and the actors will have as much influence on the audience's experience of the play as the writer. Then there are the technical people – lighting, scenery, sound and costumes all have to be created by skilled people who will all contribute to the production.

While you are writing the play you will have to immerse yourself totally in it, inhabiting its world and living the lives of its characters. Once you have finished the writing, you will have to let go of all that and hand your play over to these other people for their input. If you can't do that, then write a novel, not a play.

Rehearsals

You may or may not be welcome at rehearsals – it depends on the director, who has the final decision about everything to do with your play from the minute you hand it over. If you are invited to attend, then sit at the back and keep quiet, especially at the beginning. Actors have ways of quickly establishing their group bonds and you need to let them get on with it. Don't worry if they appear to be unfriendly at this stage – they will be very focused on learning to work with each other and the writer has nothing to contribute to this process. Once everyone has learnt that you aren't going to make a nuisance of yourself, then you should find yourself included in the discussions. Limit yourself to important points only and keep your answers brief.

Probably the best thing is to keep away from the first few rehearsals, where there will be lots of false starts and explorations of the play. Ask to attend one rehearsal when the performances are beginning to take shape, but while there are still questions that need answering. Remember that the director is in charge. Don't question their authority, and if you need to challenge what they are doing with your play, ask to speak to them in private.

Summary

In this chapter you have learnt:

- about staging requirements
- not to leave a corpse on stage
- how to behave at rehearsals.

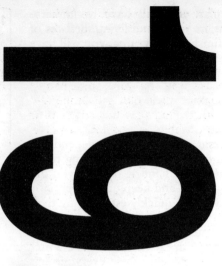

19

script layouts and submission

In this chapter you will learn:
- how to create a professional-looking script
- the different script layouts
- the dos and don'ts of sending submissions.

The most common mistake that new playwrights make is: submitting scripts which are too fussy and too elaborately presented.

L. A. Hudswell, script reader

You can write your early drafts any way you want. Some people like to be super-organized, breaking their plot into units and writing each one separately. Others find that this stifles their creativity and that they need to scribble on odd bits of paper. There are only two golden rules:

- Don't try to hold the play in your head. It won't mean anything until you get it out onto paper or computer screen. Sadly, most of us find that the play in our head is much better than the first draft that results – all we can do is polish and re-write.
- Before you show your script to anyone, put it into a professional layout. Obviously if you can manage to write straight into a proper layout you will save yourself a lot of time re-typing, or re-formatting if you use a computer.

Theatre script layout

Unlike film, television and radio, there is no one accepted standard layout for theatre scripts. There are, however, some basic rules that need to be followed. It is worth putting the effort into producing a script that looks and feels good – the first person to see it will probably be a script reader, not an actor or a director, and your task is to get them interested in your script for all the right reasons, and not because it is the scruffiest or dirtiest they have ever seen. There are some basic rules to follow.

- A script should be typed or computer printed, never handwritten.
- Use A4 size paper.
- Use 12 point size font, Arial, Times New Roman or Courier are popular fonts; don't use fancy fonts which can be difficult to read.
- Use only one side of the paper.
- Number the pages.
- Use wide margins (top, bottom, left and right) to make your script easy on the eye, and to leave space for a reader to scribble notes and queries.

- If you are using a computer you can put your name and the name of the play as a footer along the bottom of each page – use a small font size for this. The exception to this rule is if a competition requires your script to be anonymous.
- The title page should give your name, the name of the play and your contact details.
- On the next page or two provide a character list, with brief descriptions, and an equally brief description of the set and props. The details will be organized by the director and the production team, all you need to do here is give them an outline.
- Use capitals for the names of speakers and for stage directions. Some writers like to underline directions, or put them in italics, but this is not essential.
- It is most common and generally considered best practice for the name of each speaker to be set on the left hand side of the page. They can be centred, but most readers dislike this.
- Put a double space between each speech, or between speeches and stage directions, and use single spacing within speeches and stage directions.
- There are two sorts of stage directions – those that are within a speech (including those at the start of a speech) and those that are set separately, between speeches. Directions within a speech are enclosed in brackets, those between speeches are not.

Case study: script layout

Here is a short sample taken from *Freehold and Free*:

MRS G: Oh, I've just had such a shock.

FRAN: Really? Perhaps you'd better sit down.

MRS G: *(sits, and grunts with effort)* Thank you dear, I will. Could I possibly trouble you for a glass of water?

FRAN: I suppose so. Still or sparkling?

MRS G: No dear, just water, I never touch alcohol.

Fran exits to kitchen.

MRS G: *(calling)* I think your flowers are dead.

FRAN: *(off)* I'm sorry?

The direction '*Fran exits to the kitchen*' is indented so that script readers and actors running their eye down a script's left hand margin only see character names. Some writers would have put '*Fran*' in bold, to make it stand out, but this can make a script look too fussy. Simple is best when it comes to layout.

Television and radio script layout

The BBC has devised templates for radio and television script layouts, which can be downloaded from their website (see Taking It Further). The BBC Writersroom does not expect unsolicited scripts to be formatted, but they do want them to be clearly presented with double spacing.

Submissions

- Never send out your only copy of a script. Always keep a paper copy or a computer backup.
- There is no hard and fast rule about securing the pages of a script, but the best thing is probably to use a single fastener in the top left hand corner. This means the pages can be turned easily and the reader can easily remove it if they prefer loose pages (this is why the pages have to be numbered).
- Don't waste money on expensive bindings, photos or drawings of suggestions for sets and costumes or lists of possible famous actors who could be cast in your masterpiece. Doing this will mark you out as a beginner, and probably cause both irritation and mirth in the theatre. All that's needed is white paper with black print on it, and a covering letter. Keep your covering letter short and to the point. Don't make jokes ('my mum thinks it's great') or show off. If you feel you already have a good track record, then include a brief CV – one page only.
- If you want to be sure that the script has been received, then include a stamped addressed postcard – some organizations do automatically acknowledge receipt, but many don't. There is no rule about whether to include return postage; we used to, until one day a reader said 'I don't like to see return postage, it shows a lack of confidence'. If you want to be sure of getting your script back, then include the postage. Again, some organizations automatically return scripts, but not all do.
- There is a gradual move towards accepting e-mailed script submissions, but you should always ask before doing this. Ask if you can send it as an attachment, so that your layout is preserved in transit.

Summary

In this chapter you have learnt:

- how to get your play down on paper
- how to lay out scripts in various genres
- how to make a submission.

20

outlets and networking opportunities

In this chapter you will learn:
- about theatres that take unsolicited scripts
- about other outlets for new writing
- about publishing and licensing plays
- about other practical aspects of getting a play produced.

*The most common mistake that new playwrights make is:
the assumption that the reading and evaluating of scripts
by editors or producers or publishers is applied efficiently
and fairly and objectively to all by all. All it is, is a personal
response by a reader to a piece of writing. And the reader
brings to it all his personal baggage and experience, likes
and dislikes, prejudices and obsessions.*

**Tony Staveacre, writer/producer in television, radio
and theatre, author of three books on popular culture**

When you have reached the end of the final re-write you may
think that your work is over, but that is far from the case. The
play needs to find a home, and if you want to see it performed
you will have to send it out into the world to be judged. Perhaps
you are in the happy position of knowing exactly where your
play is going, in which case you may think you don't need this
chapter. But what will happen to it next? Has it got a future
after the immediate use you have for it?

Professional payments

There are an astonishing number of ways that a play can reach
an audience. However, most of them do not generate any
financial benefit for the writer. There are any number of
organizations that will take a play for free, and very few that are
able to pay. Don't assume that the former are an easy ride –
most of them have very high standards and plenty of plays to
choose from. Only you can say how important it is to you to be
paid for your writing. If you have ambitions to earn your living
as a playwright, you might have to start by working for free
before moving on to being paid.

In the commercial theatre writers are usually paid a flat fee by
negotiation. The theatre will have a standard contract. If you
have an agent they will deal with it, otherwise you will handle
it yourself. The fee is paid in instalments, the final one being due
on acceptance of the script for production. Usually there is no
guarantee in the contract that your play will actually be
performed.

Outlets for plays

Theatres

Large London theatres tend to stage plays by well-known writers, but there are a few theatres, particularly those in the provinces, that will look at unsolicited scripts. Some of these also provide a script reading service – usually for a fee to cover costs. The most important thing is to take notice of each theatre's preferences. If they ask for postal submissions only, then don't e-mail an attachment. If they ask for outlines only, then don't send a full script. If you ignore these requests, you will at best irritate the reader and at worst have your work returned unread.

It can take a long time for a script to be read and returned, so learn to be patient. In fact, start writing your next play, rather than waiting anxiously for news of the last one.

The script will probably be read by somebody on the theatre's creative team who has a lot of other jobs to do and who has landed the task of reading scripts, probably much against their will. Initially they will be asked to read through the script, and produce a short report that recommends what should happen next. (Occasionally the reader is someone from outside the theatre, contracted on a freelance basis to read scripts, but they will work in the same way.) Almost everything that they read will be rejected, and the few really interesting scripts will be passed on to someone more senior to look at. If this person also likes the play, then they will make contact with you. If geographically possible, they will ask you to come in and meet them. This is a great step forward, but don't get too excited. The chances that they want to put on your play are slight. However, they may have a scheme for new writers, or they may have a programme of low-budget lunchtime performances that you could write for. If you are offered a chance of involvement with anything like this, take it if you possibly can, even if there is no money in it, because it could lead on to other commissions. If all they are able to offer are suggestions on how you can improve your work, at least it shows they thought it was worth reading – so take note and implement their advice.

Send your script to as many theatres as you can, but pay particular attention to any theatres near where you live, because those are the ones that will offer the best chance of a foot in the door.

Rehearsed readings and script-in-hand performances

These take place in front of an audience, and in both cases the actors won't learn their lines but will hold their scripts as they perform.

- Rehearsed readings tend to be static, with actors standing or sitting as they read – rather like a radio play.
- Script-in-hand performances will include the entrances and exits and as much of the business as actors can do with their one free hand.

Case study: script-in-hand performance

Over Exposure once received a script-in-hand where the actors were willing to do every single thing, including several on-stage changes of costume. Of course since it is a comedy they were happy to get extra laughs off the awkwardness caused by having to hold the scripts.

Touring groups

The tradition of the group of touring players is far from dead. These small groups operate on shoestring budgets and many of them produce their own material. However some are interested in commissioning new work, if it can be written to their tight specifications, which usually include a small cast and a minimum of props and scenery.

Pub theatre

A lot of pubs have a performance space in the building and, depending on their customer base, may well use it for small scale drama. A local theatre group will use the space and will have some sort of financial deal with the pub owners that keeps their costs low, and touring groups may also visit. Pub theatre is usually quite adventurous and often has a loyal audience that turns out regularly expecting to be shocked, surprised or amused. Very few of these venues appear in any listing other than local newspapers, so it's a question of doing your own research. If there is a pub theatre near you, start by going to a performance – you'll get a feel for the type of play they put on, and the programme will probably have contact details for the organizer.

Amateur groups

There are over 20,000 amateur drama groups around the country, so the chances are there is one near you, and probably several. Visit your library, where they will keep a listing of all local organizations, and check out your local paper for information about performances. It's unlikely that any group will take a script from someone that they don't know, so get involved with them and learn about their needs.

You are unlikely to be paid for writing for an amateur group, but the learning experience will be invaluable. You will be able to re-write the play post-performance and you may be able to start a press cuttings file if the local paper reviews it.

Charities and special groups

Local charities will often consider putting on a performance that highlights issues around their particular cause, for instance, domestic violence. They can rarely afford to pay the writer and performers, but the experience is invaluable.

Community drama and local history

Community groups stage performances that tell the history of their village or town, and are often grateful for help with the writing. The advantage to the first-time writer is that the plot is already there, although it will need some artistic control. Again, don't expect to be paid, but do expect to learn some valuable lessons.

Dramatized pageants are similar to community drama but are performed in unusual venues, usually outside, and are often connected with a local historical event. Sometimes they tell their entire story visually, without any dialogue, or with just a narrator.

Teenagers and children

Small children usually love to perform but rarely have a long enough attention span to carry a whole play. Older children and teenagers are inclined to be more self-conscious, but most schools have a flourishing drama club. Usually an over-worked teacher writes their scripts – he or she may be more than happy to hand the task over.

Competitions

There are an astonishing number of competitions for playwrights. Information about writing competitions appears in all sorts of places – your local paper, the Internet, Arts Council newsletters and other newsletters – one good reason why it is worth joining writers' organizations.

They vary greatly both in what they cost to enter and in the rewards on offer. Entry costs vary from nothing to about £10 per play. Prizes can include small amounts of cash, reader's reports, workshops, script-in-hand or rehearsed readings, full performance (by amateur or professional actors) and publication by the competition organizers. All are useful but oddly enough cash prizes, while being a tremendous ego boost, are the least useful to a writer. Every other sort of prize offers a valuable learning experience that should be grabbed with both hands.

Any sort of performance, whether it is a full production or a rehearsed reading, will help you see your play's weaknesses and give you the opportunity for a re-write. They also give you a chance to do some networking and get to know local actors and directors.

Reader's reports are always useful and should be taken seriously. Of course they are only one anonymous person's opinion, and you will never know what level of knowledge and experience they have, but they provide you with an unusually objective response to your play on the page.

Case study: reader's report

Whatever You Want was read by somebody who didn't realize that Ray and Margaret had been completely out of touch with Dilys and Steve before the play opened, and was therefore puzzled that Margaret didn't recognize Dilys. Our first response was 'how brainless can you be' but our second was 'maybe we need to look at the exposition'.

Festivals

Most parts of the country hold one-act drama competitions, with the winners going on to the All-England One-Act Play Festival finals. Although these competitions are judging the actors, the directors and the productions, they often require new scripts. The best way to find out more about drama festivals in your area is via your local amateur drama groups. See also the useful websites in Taking It Further.

Networking and information gathering

The more involvement you have with theatre activities in your local area the more networking opportunities you will encounter, and the more information about writing opportunities you will acquire. Use the Internet also to track down information.

- **Workshops.** These provide networking opportunities, which could lead to a placement for your play. Workshops are closed events, usually consisting of a workshop leader and a group of writers who have been invited along or who have applied to join. The aim is to help develop a writer's material often through a series of exercises which stretch the imagination. They give the writer an opportunity to meet with other writers and to receive constructive criticism. They are often run by adult education centres or as part of extra mural university courses.
- **The Arts Councils.** The Arts Councils are publicly funded bodies for the promotion and support of all the arts. They are able to make grants and have their own unique criteria, so check out their websites (see Taking It Further). The application process can be very long-winded and usually requires a writer to give a lot of detail about the proposed work. It is worth being on the mailing list for your region as they usually produce a newsletter with information about both the Arts Council itself and other opportunities such as competitions and workshops.

Publication

There are a few specialized publishers (see Taking it further) who publish plays and who make scripts available for amateur performance. They handle the publicity and the licensing of the performances and pay the writer a percentage. The copyright in the play stays with the writer.

The publishers are of course careful about which plays they choose. When you send them a script, say something about its performance history, because they are unlikely to take a play that has never been performed.

Copyright

Like any other area of the law, copyright is complex, but the underlying principles are simple. You automatically own the copyright in anything you write, and if anybody performs your play or uses extracts from it without your permission then they are in breach of your copyright. Copyright continues for 70 years after the writer's death, with their estate benefiting from any payments.

There is, however, no copyright in ideas, so if somebody else writes a play that is similar to yours it will be hard to prove that the original idea was yours. In the past writers have felt the need to register their copyright, in case they ever needed to prove the date on which they wrote something. The simple way to do this is to post the play to yourself, using recorded delivery. Don't open it when it arrives, and the postmark supplies evidence of date. The Patent Office website offers good advice on copyright. Nowadays, with most writing done on a computer, which gives a start date for each file, it is possible to prove when something was first written.

In practice most of us don't need to worry about this. Most people in the industry are honest and honourable and won't attempt to steal your work. If you are particularly worried about copyright, then take legal advice.

If your play includes quotes from other people's work then you need permission if it is still in copyright.

Licensing your play

You can set up your own system for licensing your plays for amateur performance. Once a play has had one successful performance, you may well find other groups become interested, and there is nothing wrong with charging them a small fee. Draw up a simple document that shows exactly how the licence works, for instance:

> 'The fee is £25 to cover all rehearsals including the dress rehearsal and two performances, with an extra £10 per additional performance.'

Also include a date at which the licence will lapse. For instance if the group is planning an autumn production, then licence them till the end of the year. Finally, make it clear how many copies of the script you will provide. We keep our licence fees very low, but we only provide one script, and the group have to arrange photocopying.

Bear in mind that very small sums of money will be involved, and without the advice of a solicitor you can't regard this as a legal document.

If you plan to license your plays you will need to advertise them. One way of doing this is to set up your own website as we have done. It is helpful to put on it a few sample pages from each play as well as a synopsis, how many male and female parts there are and a description of the set or sets. Other ways are by advertising in theatrical magazines, but this could be an expensive option.

Getting an agent

This is a chicken and egg situation, since agents won't be terribly interested in a writer with no track record, but it can be difficult for a writer to get a track record without the help of an agent. However, it is worthwhile trying to get one because a lot of theatres will only take scripts via an agent, on the basis that the agent will have sieved out the dud scripts and will only pass on the good ones.

Approach them by letter or e-mail, stating briefly what your successes so far are, and offering to send a sample script.

Proposals, treatments, outlines and synopses

Instead of being asked for a complete script you may be asked to send one of the above. There is a lot of overlap between these terms and they are often used interchangeably:

- A proposal is usually written before the play. It is a description of what the play would be like if it were to be written.
- A treatment is similar to a proposal, and the word is usually used to describe a proposed film rather than a play.
- An outline can sometimes have the same meaning as proposal or treatment, or it can mean a short (one sentence or one paragraph) description of a play already written.
- A synopsis is a description of a play that has already been written, and is usually one side of an A4 sheet, although you

may be asked for a longer synopsis by some organizations. Usually synopses should be workman-like rather than clever pieces of writing in themselves, although occasionally circumstances might demand that you produce a really eye-catching synopsis. Don't be tempted to keep any secrets, especially about the ending – the whole point is to explain the play.

Writing these is a challenge, since they will be used to sell the idea of your play to people who aren't prepared to look at complete scripts. If you can make your play sound interesting enough, you will be asked to send the whole script.

Top tip

Even if you don't have an immediate need for a synopsis, writing one can be a useful exercise. Start by describing the play in a short sentence, then a paragraph, then a page. The discipline of summarizing the whole thing in a sentence will really focus your mind on what is at the core of the play.

Coping with difficulties

Rejection

Most people worry about rejection, but it is part and parcel of playwriting – everyone, even the most famous playwright, has had their plays rejected at one time or another. Remember it is only a piece of your writing which is being rejected, not you as a person. If it is really worrying you then write under a pseudonym, then the rejection applies to your alter ego not you.

Use rejection as a positive tool. If you are lucky enough to be given constructive feedback with the rejection, then take note of it. It is easy to believe that what we have written is perfect and cannot be improved, but when someone else looks at it totally objectively they will see the flaws. We know from bitter experience that what we thought we were saying wasn't what other people were reading.

If it is just a standard rejection letter, perhaps it is because you sent your play to the wrong type of theatre. Not all theatre listings say what type of play the theatre specializes in. If you pick the wrong one look on it as bad luck not a rejection.

Remember, theatres, agents and publishers receive hundreds of unsolicited scripts and usually do not have the time to say why they are returning it. If you are still convinced that your play has merit send it somewhere else straightaway. And if that fails, send it somewhere else. Stamina is needed for getting your play placed as well as for writing it.

Top tip

Don't keep sending out the same copy which could start looking dog-eared after going through the post several times. The play reader will instantly realize it has been doing the rounds and will have a negative feeling before they even turn the first page. Sometimes just printing off a new front page can freshen up a script.

Criticism

If your play is performed, whether professionally or by amateurs, the media critics may well make some comments on it. Always take what is said with a pinch of salt, whether the comments are favourable or damning. Remember, everyone who watches your play, including the critics, brings with them their own experiences and prejudices – so total agreement is rare. Learn what you can from the critical comments and put the good ones in your cuttings file.

Loss of self-confidence

This is not confined to new writers, it can happen to anyone. Hurtful comments by critics can be demoralising. But remember, it is easier to criticize something which someone else has written, it is much harder to write something original. Even if no one likes what you have written, at least you had a go at writing it and you should be proud of that fact. Like getting back on a horse after you have been thrown off, learn from your mistakes; try writing something different, but keep going.

Summary

In this chapter you have learnt:

- where to place a play
- about the importance of networking
- how to submit a script
- how to handle rejection and criticism
- to never give up.

21

putting on
your own play

In this chapter you will learn:
- about organizing a
  performance
- about the Edinburgh Fringe.

The most common mistake that new playwrights make is: not putting themselves in the position of the audience. Whatever the motivation for writing the play, the piece is being written to be performed before an audience. Make sure your audience is always 'on the hook'.

Ray Cooney, playwright

There are many reasons why a play is rejected and poor quality is only one of them. Commercial theatres have to be sure of a play attracting reasonably large audiences so they tend to go for tried and tested writers who are well known to the public. Smaller companies may not have the resources to mount your play, and amateurs may find it too challenging. If you have absolute faith in the quality of your piece, and if you have taken to heart and acted on all the feedback, then consider producing it yourself.

To mount your own production you will need:

- time
- energy
- money.

It is perfectly possible to put on your own production of your play. We know, because we have done it – we put on our own production of *Over Exposure*. It is not, however, for the faint hearted or anybody without a lot of time, energy and organizational skills. Think of the time and effort it took to write the script, multiply that by ten and you will be somewhere close to what it takes.

It is surprisingly possible to keep costs very low, but it can't be done without a certain amount of cash. For that reason you should start by costing out the various aspects of the production before deciding whether to go ahead. Take into account the worse case scenario, such as the leading actor falling ill as the curtain goes up and you having to refund all the ticket money. Can you afford to lose the money you have invested? If the answer is yes then producing your own play can be a rewarding business – probably not financially, but in many other ways.

Your budget will tell you whether you can afford to pay the people who become involved in the production. If you are planning to pay, contact Equity (the actors' union) who will tell you what the current minimum rates are. We offered to share out all the profits once our expenses were covered. Although there was no guarantee of any profits, our actors and director were all willing to meet their own incidental expenses. We knew from this that they really loved *Over Exposure* and wanted to be in it. We also knew that if a fully paid acting job came up they would take it, so we had other actors as backups. This is accepted in the industry, although it is not considered good form to leave a production if there is less than a month to go before the performances.

Resources

Performance space

There are plenty of affordable performance spaces in village halls, community centres and pubs. Check out the cost of hire for the number of nights you require. Consider the location of the venue too – a remote village hall might be cheap, but will anyone turn out? Timing can affect price, with the summer being a quiet time for most venues. We chose a city centre pub theatre in the early summer. It gave us the advantage of a core audience who were in the habit of seeing most of the productions there. However, popular venues get booked up well in advance so be prepared to make a provisional booking, which will probably incur a deposit.

Director

If you have the experience, by all means direct the play yourself, but otherwise look for a director. This is where networking is helpful. Because we had already had some success in competitions, we had got to know quite a few local actors and directors who we could approach.

You may already know a gifted amateur, but it is worth contacting colleges and drama schools in your area to see if they run courses for directors. They are often mature students with a lot of theatre knowledge and they will be looking for directing opportunities. For this reason, and if they are enthusiastic about your piece, they may be willing to direct it for free. If it is hard to find people who like your play well enough to commit to it, then it probably isn't ready for performance yet. Go back to the re-write stage and put off your production for a while.

Actors

It is usual for the director to be responsible for casting, but since you will be the producer as well as the writer you can expect a certain amount of involvement. Both you and the director should use all your contacts amongst amateur and professional actors, and students, to get the best cast you can. Again, they may have their own reasons for working for free, since any professional performance goes on their CV.

Rehearsal space

The venue will only be available to you for the dress rehearsal and the actual performances. The rest of the time the director and cast will need access to a warm, dry, bare room for rehearsals. Your living room almost certainly won't be large enough or empty enough, so look around for free spaces. If any of your cast and crew are students, they may be able to persuade their college to let you have use of a room. Rooms in pubs can often be quite cheap to hire because the pub knows that they will be taking money over the bar and rehearsing can be thirsty work.

Scenery

If you are going to have scenery, it needs to be professionally done. Again you may be able to make contact with a student of scenery design. Since our venue didn't have much space for scenery we played to black curtains.

Costumes

Nothing marks out an amateur production more than lack of coherent costume design. Costume design is a speciality, and proper costume design is expensive, so again it is worth trying to find a student or a gifted amateur. We didn't manage either. *Over Exposure* is set in the 1970s, and between the cast and the charity shops we managed to find enough kipper ties and tank tops, but we always knew it was a weak spot in our production.

Props

If your play calls for special or complicated props you will probably have to pay for them. Otherwise, make yourself responsible for props, but ask around the cast and crew for anything you can't find. Occasionally local businesses such as furniture shops will lend you props, in return for an advert in your programme.

Lighting and sound effects

It is best to engage a professional (or a student) to design your lighting. Once the lighting board is set up it is usually fairly straightforward to operate – in fact ours was run by the director. Sound effects require someone reliable with a good sense of timing. The technical rehearsal will probably have to take place on the same day as the dress rehearsal. Keep your requirements as simple as possible – if you are over-ambitious you are more likely to have mistakes in performance.

Insurance

Ask the venue what insurance they have in place – ask to see a copy of the policy. If your actors are members of Equity then they will have a measure of insurance, so that if one of them accidentally causes an injury to a member of the audience there is cover. Because one of our actors was at the start of his career and still had amateur status we had to take out an extra insurance for the week of our run. It virtually doubled our budget.

Videoing

If it is possible, record a performance on video or DVD. The quality probably won't be good enough for anything other than helping you remember what you need to do for the post-performance re-write, but it is invaluable to have a record of the performance.

Manpower

- **Backstage.** Small venues will not provide any backstage staff and you will need to assemble a team. Talk to the director and cast first, and see what they are willing to do. In our case each cast member was happy to take responsibility for their own props.
- **Front of house.** Again small venues often expect you to run front of house yourself. Friends and family will probably volunteer, but make sure they understand that they need to be soberly dressed, polite and helpful. They should familiarize themselves with the venue beforehand. If you are using a hall with a car park you may need a steward or two to persuade people to park tidily.

Flyers, programmes and tickets

As soon as you know the production is going ahead, organize a single design for the front cover of the programme and the flyers. Aim for a simple eye-catching design that can be easily printed on a home computer, or run off in a copy shop. By using the same image on all the material you will create an identity for your play.

Flyers are small posters, usually A5 size, that contain the basic information about the performance:

- dates
- times
- ticket costs
- website
- box office phone number.

The programme should contain a brief biography for each cast member and the director, with contact details if they wish. They will want to use your play as a chance to demonstrate their ability, and they will undoubtedly invite their own theatre contacts along to watch – the programme is a publicity tool for them. Don't forget to include something about yourself.

You can also include in the programme a short questionnaire for the audience, to gauge their response to the play.

Tickets can also be run off on a home computer.

Publicity

There are two kinds of publicity:

- the pre-show publicity you need to sell tickets
- using your production as a vehicle to promote your writing talents.

Before you start selling tickets, work out what the box office arrangement will be. Small venues don't usually have the facility for a box office, and the best course is to publicize a phone number for ticket sales.

Of course you will sell some tickets to your friends and family, but unless you are only playing one or two nights this won't be enough. Our venue had a minimum week's booking (Sunday to Sunday), with plays usually running Tuesday through Saturday – five nights, so we needed to do a lot of publicity.

Pre-show publicity

Start with your local media and papers. Send out a press release. Try to give them a ready made story about you and your play. Newspapers need an 'angle' before they are prepared to give free publicity, so try to think of something newsworthy such as a plea to the public for an unusual prop. Offer them a photo opportunity and don't forget to include your contact number. If the paper can't send a photographer, take some good digital photos yourself and send them to the paper – if they have a space they will probably use them.

You will probably get a call from the advertising department asking if you want to advertise the play. We didn't, because we couldn't afford it. We did get a listing in a magazine where it was free. Also send the press release to your local television and radio stations, and be prepared to go along to be interviewed. If you are too shy, ask your leading actor to do it.

Run off as many flyers as you can afford, and try to get them displayed all round the local area. A5 size is small enough that people will often allow you to put one up, where they may not have space for a large poster. Ask in shops where you are known, libraries, schools, colleges, offices. Be prepared for a lot of refusals. Where possible leave a pile of flyers for individuals to take away with them.

If you have a website, download the flyer onto it. Contact everybody you know with information about the play. Never mind how far away they live – they may have a holiday or a business trip to your area.

Self-promotion

Now turn your attention to promoting yourself as a writer, because the production gives you a chance to show your playwriting skills to producers and directors who may be interested in producing your play themselves or who may offer you an opportunity to write something especially for them.

Offer a pair of free tickets to every theatre in your area – and make it a big area because again, somebody might be passing through. Before you make the offer, phone each theatre and find out the name of the Creative Director so that you can address the offer personally. Extend the offer to anyone else you can think of – radio and television companies, production companies etc. Trawl the Yellow Pages. Finally don't forget the Press. Find out the name of the theatre critic on every local publication and send them tickets – don't just offer this time. You want to make it as easy as possible for them to review your play.

The result of all this hard work for us was that we sold so many tickets we had to add an extra performance. We also had a good review in a local daily paper which was helpful when we wanted to get the play published.

Performance and after

Chances are you will find yourself busy during the performances, but try to sit through at least one full performance. You will have already watched the play in the dress rehearsal, now is the time to watch the audience and learn from their reactions. Eavesdrop in the interval and as they are leaving.

Top tip

Remember to buy all the local papers and check for reviews, and keep copies of all of them.

Post performance

You will be responsible for clearing up the venue after the last performance. The venue will tell you if it needs to be done that night, or if you can come back the next day. Get together as many people as possible for this tedious chore.

Re-writes

There is nothing like watching your play performed to highlight the parts that do work and more importantly those that don't work. Immediately after the production has finished pull together everything you have learned, including feedback from the audience, the director and the actors, and make the necessary adjustments to your script.

Case study: post-performance re-write

We carried out a major overhaul of the opening of *Over Exposure*, which we could see needed more action. We also incorporated all the extra pieces of dialogue and business the actors came up with and got rid of those bits that either weren't necessary to the plot or slowed the action down.

Edinburgh Fringe

The Edinburgh Fringe offers amazing opportunities for a writer with the nerve and energy to engage with it. It is a huge event, taking place in numerous venues in and around Edinburgh for three weeks each August. There is no Creative Director to pick and choose who gets the chance to showcase their work – anybody can take a play to Edinburgh as long as they can find actors and a venue. In addition, over the years the Edinburgh Fringe has turned into a sort of busman's holiday for all the London-based media people, so that it is probably the best chance for a theatre scout or a television producer to see your work unsolicited. It is also an opportunity for networking, since you will find yourself rubbing shoulders with them in the audience, and in bars and restaurants.

We would recommend that you see this as a long-term project, as there is no substitute for the experience of visiting the Fringe as a spectator first, with a view to taking a play for following year. Use your trip to enjoy as many performances as possible and to check out the venues – these range from tiny rooms seating 20 or less to huge concert halls.

Work for the Fringe starts early, and you have to register your desire to be part of the Fringe early in the year. You will be sent a pack that explains how it all works and you take it from there. One tip is to book both your venue and your accommodation as early as possible – if you are really confident, book them both during your first trip ready for a production the following August.

Most small productions only run for one of the weeks and it is probably best not to try for more than this as it is extremely exhausting. You will have to do a vast amount of organization both beforehand and during the week in Edinburgh. You will need a cast who are willing to travel to Edinburgh, a director ditto, and transport for the costumes, props and scenery. As well as rehearsing in advance you should try to have at least one full performance pre-Edinburgh, so that you can re-write if necessary and take something really slick to the Fringe.

Summary

In this chapter you have learnt:

- that it is possible to put on your own production
- that you will need to be involved in every aspect
- that you can then take your play to the Edinburgh Fringe.

Theatres

Birmingham Repertory Theatre Ltd
Centenary Square
Broad Street
Birmingham, B1 2EP
0121 245 2045
info@birmingham-rep.co.uk

Approach by e-mail. No script reading service.

Druid Theatre Company
Flood St
Galway
Ireland
+353 91 568 660
info@druidtheatre.com
http://www.druidtheatre.com

Hardcopy only of full-length finished play which will be read and considered by a reading panel. We consider plays for production and can't offer individual detailed criticism of each play we receive.

Hull Truck
Spring Street
Hull, HU2 8RW
01482 224 800
admin@hulltruck.co.uk
www.hulltruck.co.uk

Hull Truck Theatre offers a script reading service, which is free of charge. Please submit by post only. Scripts should bound and single spaced. Please enclose a letter of introduction which includes any relevant information, a half-page synopsis, and a stamped addressed envelope for its return. Submissions should be addressed to: Steven Jon Atkinson, Literary Development Manager.

Liverpool Everyman and Playhouse Theatres
13 Hope Street
Liverpool, L1 9BH
literary@everymanplayhouse.com
www.everymanplayhouse.com

Extensive Playwright Support Programme. We read unsolicited script submissions (full-length, stage plays only) and offer dramaturgical feedback on all submissions. Writers please look at the kind of work we do to see if their style of work would suit these theatres.

Live Theatre
27 Broad Chare
Quayside
Newcastle-upon-Tyne, NE1 3DQ
0191 261 2694
info@live.org.uk

Postal or e-mail enquiries, free script reading service. Send two unbound copies of your script to: Script Reading Service, New Writing Department at the above address.

Northern Stage
Barras Bridge
Newcastle-upon-Tyne, NE1 7RH
0191 232 3366
info@northernstage.com

We don't offer a script reading service, and also don't accept unsolicited scripts. Preferred approach is by e-mail.

Northumberland Theatre Company
The Playhouse
Bondgate Without
Alnwick
Northumberland, NE66 1PQ
01665 602 586
admin@ntc-touringtheatre.co.uk

Contact by letter or e-mail but please post scripts with SAE for return. We will always read unsolicited work but it can take between six to nine months (or more) to read and return. Always look at the website and find out more about the company and its work before submitting scripts. Ideally see a show! It is extremely unlikely that we will produce non-commissioned scripts but if we were to like your style this could lead to a commission.

Octagon Theatre
Howell Croft South
Bolton, BL1 1SB
01204 529 407
info@octagonbolton.co.uk

Contact North West Playwrights who operate our script reading service: 0161 237 1978. We do not accept unsolicited scripts.

Out of Joint
7 Thane Works
Thane Villas
London, N7 7NU
020 7609 0207
alex@outofjoint.co.uk
www.outofjoint.co.uk

Contact by post with short covering letter to Alexandra Roberts, Literary Manager. Please enclose SAE if you would like your script returned. Your script will be read by a member of the department and feedback will be sent, if appropriate, within 12 weeks. Please look at our website before submitting your play. Although we aim to read most of the plays that are sent to us, anything particularly unsuitable will not be read.

Polka Theatre
240 The Broadway
Wimbledon
London, SW19 1SB
Box Office: 020 8543 4888
info@polkatheatre.com
www.polkatheatre.com

Send synopsis and five pages of dialogue to Associate Director, New Writing, at the address above, a full script will be requested if the play/idea is right for Polka. Happy to read unsolicited scripts and run a development programme for new writing called Playgrounding. Polka Theatre is one of the few venues in the country devoted to children and young people. New writing for children and young people is at the heart of our work. Each year we hope to commission at least three major new works across the age range 0–16 years from both established and new writers.

Solent People's Theatre
Bedhampton Arts Centre
Bedhampton
Havant
Hants, PO9 3ET
02392 423 399
brendon@solentpeoplestheatre.com

Approach in writing with abstract and scene sample. No script reading service. Our work from 2007–9 will focus almost exclusively on issues surrounding democracy and economic citizenship.

Theatre Centre London
Shoreditch Town Hall
380 Old Street
London, EC1V 9LT
admin@theatre-centre.co.uk
www.theatre-centre.co.uk

Send examples of your work with a covering letter saying why you think you would be a suitable writer for Theatre Centre. No script reading service. As we have no dedicated script readers, responding to unsolicited material takes a long time. We advise you getting to know our work thoroughly before getting in touch. Try to see our productions and visit the website to find out what is coming up. Likewise invite us to see your work. Theatre Centre rarely produces extant plays. We prefer to follow an idea from its inception to staging through our in-house development process.

The Bush Theatre
Shepherds Bush Green
London, W12 8QS
020 7602 3703
info@bushtheatre.co.uk
www.bushtheatre.co.uk/writers.html

We accept hard copies (not e-mails) of scripts that are full-length works (80+ minutes). Please send them for the attention of our Literary Manager at the above address. We are only able to return scripts that include postage-paid envelopes. The reading process takes approximately four months, and we try to offer constructive feedback if the script is not something we feel we could develop further here.

The Ramshorn Theatre
98 Ingram Street
Glasgow, G1 1ES
0141 552 3489
ramshorn.theatre@strath.ac.uk

Check first, to see if we are accepting scripts. No script reading service.

Unicorn Theatre for Children
147 Tooley Street
More London
London, SE1 2HZ
020 7645 0500
artistic@unicorntheatre.com

We do not read unsolicited scripts and we only commission writers whose work is familiar to us. If you are a writer who would like to be considered for work with Unicorn at some point, please send us the following with your contact details: a short statement describing why you would like to write for Unicorn; and your CV, if appropriate, or a summary of your relevant experience. Please do not send us a script at this point but you can include a synopsis and a scene. Please also let us know if you have work produced that you would like us to come and see.

Please send all material, by post only, to: Rhona Foulis, Assistant to the Artistic Team. We cannot accept material by e-mail or fax.

Yvonne Arnaud Theatre
Millbrook
Guildford,GU1 3UX
01483 440077
yat@yvonne-arnaud.co.uk

Contact by letter or e-mail only (no unsolicited scripts except by arrangement). No script reading service.

Agents

Brie Burkeman
14 Neville Court
Abbey Road
London, NW8 9DD
0870 199 5002
brie.burkeman@mail.com

Short letter with self-addressed stamped reply envelope or initial short enquiry only via e-mail. Unsolicited e-mail attachments will be deleted without opening. Please follow submission guidelines in the Writers' Handbook and/or the Writers' & Artists' Yearbook.

MBA Literary Agents Ltd
62 Grafton Way
London, W1T 5DW
020 7387 2076
agent@mbalit.co.uk
www.mbalit.co.uk

Please see the advice on our website under Personnel.

The Sharland Organization
The Manor House
Manor Street
Raunds
Northamptonshire, NN9 6JW
01933 626 600
tsoshar@aol.com

Initial approach by e-mail or letter. No script reading service. Plays straight or comedy and musicals.

Competitions

Derek Lomas Playwriting Competition, Wellington Theatre Company
c/o Tim Crowson
3 Bush Close
Wellington
Telford
Shropshire
01952 242 415
tim_crowson@yahoo.co.uk
www.belfreytheatre.com

Competition is run every two years, i.e. 2009, 2011. Rules and prizes can be seen on the website.

International Playwriting Festival
Warehouse Theatre
Dingwall Road
Croydon, CR0 2NF
020 8688 6699
info@warehousetheatre.co.uk
www.warehousetheatre.co.uk

This is an annual competition for full-length unperformed plays. The deadline for entries is 30 June. Selected plays are showcased during a festival weekend in November.

The Windsor Fringe Marriott Award for New Drama Writing
Suite 640
24–28 St Leonard's Road
Windsor
Berks, SL4 3BB
01753 863 218
ann.trewartha@btinternet.com
www.windsorfringe.co.uk

Unpublished one-act plays from amateur playwrights. The competition is run annually with a closing date in March. Nine plays are performed with a cash prize for the winner.

Awards

Verity Bargate Award
Soho Theatre and Writers' Centre
21 Dean Street
London, W1D 3NE
writers@sohotheatre.com
www.sohotheatre.com

This is a biennial award made to a writer of a new and unperformed full-length play. The prize is the option to produce the play at the Soho Theatre. Restricted to writers with two or less professional productions to their credit.

Publishers

Jasper Publishing Ltd
115 Harlestone Road
Northampton, NN5 7AQ
01604 590 315.
Info@jasperpublishing.com
www.jasperpublishing.com

Samuel French Ltd
52 Fitzroy Street
London, W1T 5JR
020 7387 9373
theatre@samuelfrench-london.co.uk

We are prepared to consider full-length plays for publication only if they have been successfully produced in the professional theatre. However, we will read one-act plays on the basis of a well-reviewed amateur production. Samuel French Ltd acquire performing rights in the titles we publish. An introductory letter or e-mail should be sent to us in the first instance.

Other organizations

Arts Council of England
14 Great Peter Street
London, SW1P 3NQ
0845 300 6200
enquiries@artscouncil.org.uk

Drama Association of Wales
The Old Library
Singleton Road
Splott
Cardiff, CF24 2ET
029 2945 2200
aled.daw@virgin.net

A service available to all writers, not just those living in Wales. The script reading service currently costs £15 per script. For this you get a critique from an expert with experience in the fields of writing, directing and academia. The written critique you receive is not edited in any way and is anonymous. The service takes up to two months from receipt of your play to the issue of your critical review.

If you get a 'rave' critique or a strong recommendation from the reviewer, your script will automatically be passed to DAW Publications for consideration.

An annual competition is held drawing in between 100 and 150 scripts. The competition, sponsored by Barclays, is for one-act plays of between 20 and 50 minutes playing time. The competition format is reviewed annually looking at different themes, genres and markets.

The DAW has run a play script library service for nearly 70 years. We now hold the world's largest specialist drama lending library – if it was published in the UK since 1900 we should have a copy. We are the UK Reading Room for Playwrights Canada Press and hold scripts published by all UK publishers and most international houses publishing in English. Play scripts are available for hire from DAW at ridiculously cheap rates ranging from 32p to 47p per week.

Hall for Cornwall
Back Quay
Truro
Cornwall, TR1 2LL
01872 262 465
annac@hallforcornwall.org.uk
www.hallforcornwall.org.uk

Opportunities for playwrights across the south-west at every career stage. Maybe you have just written your first ever script and want support and guidance, or maybe you're an established playwright who seeks some specialist contact. Either way, we'd love to hear from you. We don't run a writers group but offer an ongoing mentoring and support scheme for individuals, as well as producing a range of special group events each year and training for individual writers. The best way to start a relationship with us is to send us an example of your work. We not only read stage plays but also offer free written feedback within four months. Find out more by contacting Anna Coombs, Head of Projects on 01872 321964 or e-mailing annac@hallforcornwall.org.uk.

New Writing South
9 Jew Street
Brighton, BN2 1FG
01273 735 353
enquiries@newwritingsouth.com
www.newwritingsouth.com

Workshops, support and development opportunities for all creative writers in the south-east, including a vibrant programme for playwrights. For further information, including current programme of events, check out the website or e-mail or phone us.

NODA National Operatic and Dramatic Association
58–60 Lincoln Street
Peterborough, PE1 2RZ
0870 770 2480
everyone@noda.org.uk
www.noda.org.uk

Southwest Scriptwriters

Southwest Scriptwriters meets regularly at Bristol Old Vic to read and discuss members' scripts for screen, stage, television and radio – and to help promote that work to a wider audience. For more information, visit www.southwest-scriptwriters.co.uk.

The Arts Council of Wales
9 Museum Place
Cardiff, CF10 3NX
029 2037 6508
info@artswales.org.uk

The Arts Council of Wales is accountable to the Welsh Assembly Government for administering government funding of the arts in Wales, and to Parliament through the Secretary of State for Culture, Media and Sport for the distribution of National Lottery funds to the arts in Wales. For more detailed information about available funds contact Arts Council of Wales local offices: Cardiff 029 2037 6525; Carmarthen 01267 234 258; Colwyn Bay 01492 533 440.

Radio and television

BBC Writersroom
The Development Manager
BBC Writersroom, 1st Floor
Grafton House
379–81 Euston Road
London, NW1 3AU

For further information on submissions, competitions and advice go to www.bbc.co.uk.

Recommended reading

Books

Perrett, G. (1990) *Comedy Writing Step By Step*, Samuel French.
The basics of comedy writing.

George, K. (1994) *Playwriting: The First Workshop*, Butterworth Heinemann.

Argyle, M. (1981) *Bodily Communication*, Methuen.
How to recognize body language.

McKee, R. (1999) *Story*, Methuen.
Aimed at screenwriters, but contains a wealth of information relevant to all forms of storytelling.

Horstmann, R. (1991) *Writing For Radio*, A&C Black.

Gooch, S. (2001) *Writing A Play*, A&C Black.
Academic approach to the subject.

Reference books

Writers' and Artists' Yearbook, A&C Black. Annually.

The Writers' Handbook, Macmillan. Annually.

The Community Arts Directory 2002, available from Platform Publications Ltd, 020 7636 4343. Handbook for amateur drama.

Contacts, The Spotlight. Annually. Comprehensive theatrical handbook.

Hartnoll, P. (1972) ed., *The Concise Oxford Companion To The Theatre*, Oxford Press.

Bordman, G. *The Concise Oxford Companion To The American Theatre,* Oxford Press.

Magazines

Amateur Stage
A monthly magazine available from Platform Publications Ltd., 020 7636 4343.

Writernet bulletin
A magazine produced by www.writernet.org.

Useful websites

www.AmaDrama.co.uk
Free pantomime songs.

www.amdram.co.uk
Free website for the amateur theatre community.

www.bbc.co.uk/writersroom
For all information on writing for the BBC.

en.wikipedia.org/
Biographies of all major playwrights and short synopsizes of most major plays.

www.gabwhacker.com/xwp/bluequill/
Tips on dramatic writing.

www.hampsteadtheatre.com
Prepared to look at new writing.

www.itc-arts.org
A practical guide for writers and companies.

www.patent.gov.uk
For information on copyright.

plays4theatre.site-street.net
Will look at unsolicited scripts and publishes plays on line, also loans play scripts.

www.playwrightsstudio.co.uk
Works with playwrights and holds competitions.

www.Scotland.ideasfactory.com
Mentors new playwrights, holds workshops, helps with developing new scripts.

www.societyofauthors.net
Gives help and information.

www.stageplays.com
Sells play and musical scripts.

www.stratfordeast.com
The Theatre Royal Stratford East reads scripts and runs writers' groups.

www.theatrecrafts.com
Gives technical advice.

www.vcu.edu/artweb/playwriting
Detailed breakdown of the dramatic structure.

www.writersdigest.com
An American site with lots of information.

www.writersguild.org.uk
The Writers Guild of Great Britain.

www.writing.org.uk
Useful advice on writing.

Courses

www3.open.ac.uk
Open University courses on how to start writing plays.

www.arvonfoundation.org
Short residential courses in playwriting in Devon, Inverness-shire, Shropshire and West Yorkshire.

www.bham.ac.uk
Birmingham University, Playwriting Studies course.

www.everymanplayhouse.com
Information on master classes, workshops and new writing initiatives.

www.lifelong.ed.ac.uk
Edinburgh University, courses in playwriting.

www.londonmet.ac.uk/
London Metropolitan University, courses in scriptwriting.

www.rts.org.uk
Useful advice on writing for television.

www.tynewydd.org
Week-long residential courses in playwriting.

www.writewords.org.uk/ runs
Courses on writing for the theatre.

www.wss.org.uk
Week-long residential courses in Swanwick near Derby.

Plays by Ann Gawthorpe and Lesley Bown

Don't get your Vicars in a Twist (pages 127, 128, 133)
Freehold and Free (pages 35, 141, 188)
Living Doll (pages 12, 167)
Over Exposure (see index)
Short, Back and Lies (page 138)
The Tour Starts Here (pages 141, 171–2)
Whatever You Want (see index)
For more information see Ann and Lesley's website at
www.freewebs.co.uk/womenwhatwrite/

Some of their plays are published by Jasper, 01604 590315,
info@jasperpublishing.com, www.jasperpublishing.com

Beryl is tidying her desk ready to leave the office. Mel is sitting at a computer terminal. The clock on the wall shows 16:55.

BERYL: *(putting on her coat)* I'm leaving now Melanie.

MEL: Okey dokey. Have a good time.

BERYL: Actually I have to get to the doctor's, they wouldn't give me a later appointment.

MEL: You aren't ill or nothing?

Phone rings and Beryl answers it.

BERYL: Yes Mr Hubert ... oh, well, I haven't ... yes of course right away.

She puts down the phone and takes off her coat.

MEL: What did he want?

BERYL: His meeting's been moved forward. He wants those figures by nine tomorrow.

MEL: Do it first thing, it'll be OK.

BERYL: No, we need to finish it now. Just show me what I have to do.

MEL: Just click on that. *(She stares at the computer screen.)* Oh for crying out loud.

BERYL: What, what's happened?

MEL: It's crashed. It's no good Beryl, we might as well go home.

BERYL: Can't you do something?

MEL: No. *(Sudden thought.)* Yes I can. *(She dials a number, speaks into the phone.)* Stevie? Hi, it's Mel, ummm I got a problem ... *(giggles)* no not like that ... me computer's crashed ... can you come and look at it ... like now. Ciao, Stevie. *(She replaces the phone and turns to Beryl.)* Steve's coming up to have a look.

BERYL: But he's not IT support. I'll phone them, they can't all have gone home.

MEL: They'll take forever, you know what they're like. Steve's a fast worker.

BERYL: He does know about computers?

MEL: Well he's good with his hands *(beat)* so they tell me anyway.

Steve enters and looks at Mel's screen.

STEVE: What have you done to it? Shift yourself then.

Mel gets up, Steve sits in her place and starts typing. Mel hangs over his shoulder.

BERYL: Will this take long?

MEL: *(to Steve)* It's alright, there's no rush.

BERYL: We have some urgent figures to finish and I have to get away.

STEVE: *(to Mel)* No wonder it crashed, how many games have you downloaded?

MEL: Not that many.

STEVE: All this equipment needs updating, it came out of the Ark.

MEL: *(laughing)* Probably blow up one day.

Steve continues typing.

STEVE: Is that what you were working on?

He gets up and Mel sits down.

MEL: There you are Beryl, panic over. Thanks Steve, you're a honey.

STEVE: I aim to please.

BERYL: Could we just get this finished please?

The phone rings on Beryl's desk. She answers it.

BERYL: Yes Mr Hubert, I have them right here. *(She hangs up.)*

MEL: *(to Steve)* You off home then or do you fancy a drink?

STEVE: Could do.

They start to move off stage.

BERYL: You can't go yet. How do I print them off?

Mel comes back.

MEL: *(irritably)* For goodness sake, just click on that.

Mel and Steve exit. Beryl clicks, the printer makes a strange noise, smoke pours out of it. Phone starts ringing.

BERYL: *(calling)* Mel, Steve, come back!

Beryl takes a fire extinguisher and sprays the printer. She then picks up the phone.

BERYL: I'm sorry Mr Hubert, but the figures have gone up in smoke ... you will need to buy a new system ... no, I will deal with it in the morning ... I have to leave now because I have a doctor's appointment.

index

teach yourself®

From Advanced Sudoku to Zulu, you'll find everything you need in the **teach yourself** range, in books, on CD and on DVD.

Visit **www.teachyourself.co.uk** for more details.

Advanced Sudoku and Kakuro
Afrikaans
Alexander Technique
Algebra
Ancient Greek
Applied Psychology
Arabic
Aromatherapy
Art History
Astrology
Astronomy
AutoCAD 2004
AutoCAD 2007
Ayurveda
Baby Massage and Yoga
Baby Signing
Baby Sleep
Bach Flower Remedies
Backgammon
Ballroom Dancing
Basic Accounting
Basic Computer Skills
Basic Mathematics
Beauty
Beekeeping
Beginner's Arabic Script
Beginner's Chinese Script
Beginner's Dutch

Beginner's French
Beginner's German
Beginner's Greek
Beginner's Greek Script
Beginner's Hindi
Beginner's Italian
Beginner's Japanese
Beginner's Japanese Script
Beginner's Latin
Beginner's Mandarin Chinese
Beginner's Portuguese
Beginner's Russian
Beginner's Russian Script
Beginner's Spanish
Beginner's Turkish
Beginner's Urdu Script
Bengali
Better Bridge
Better Chess
Better Driving
Better Handwriting
Biblical Hebrew
Biology
Birdwatching
Blogging
Body Language
Book Keeping
Brazilian Portuguese

Bridge
British Empire, The
British Monarchy from Henry VIII, The
Buddhism
Bulgarian
Business Chinese
Business French
Business Japanese
Business Plans
Business Spanish
Business Studies
Buying a Home in France
Buying a Home in Italy
Buying a Home in Portugal
Buying a Home in Spain
C++
Calculus
Calligraphy
Cantonese
Car Buying and Maintenance
Card Games
Catalan
Chess
Chi Kung
Chinese Medicine
Christianity
Classical Music
Coaching
Cold War, The
Collecting
Computing for the Over 50s
Consulting
Copywriting
Correct English
Counselling
Creative Writing
Cricket
Croatian
Crystal Healing
CVs
Czech
Danish
Decluttering
Desktop Publishing
Detox

Digital Home Movie Making
Digital Photography
Dog Training
Drawing
Dream Interpretation
Dutch
Dutch Conversation
Dutch Dictionary
Dutch Grammar
Eastern Philosophy
Electronics
English as a Foreign Language
English for International Business
English Grammar
English Grammar as a Foreign Language
English Vocabulary
Entrepreneurship
Estonian
Ethics
Excel 2003
Feng Shui
Film Making
Film Studies
Finance for Non-Financial Managers
Finnish
First World War, The
Fitness
Flash 8
Flash MX
Flexible Working
Flirting
Flower Arranging
Franchising
French
French Conversation
French Dictionary
French Grammar
French Phrasebook
French Starter Kit
French Verbs
French Vocabulary
Freud
Gaelic

Gardening
Genetics
Geology
German
German Conversation
German Grammar
German Phrasebook
German Verbs
German Vocabulary
Globalization
Go
Golf
Good Study Skills
Great Sex
Greek
Greek Conversation
Greek Phrasebook
Growing Your Business
Guitar
Gulf Arabic
Hand Reflexology
Hausa
Herbal Medicine
Hieroglyphics
Hindi
Hindi Conversation
Hinduism
History of Ireland, The
Home PC Maintenance and
  Networking
How to DJ
How to Run a Marathon
How to Win at Casino Games
How to Win at Horse Racing
How to Win at Online Gambling
How to Win at Poker
How to Write a Blockbuster
Human Anatomy & Physiology
Hungarian
Icelandic
Improve Your French
Improve Your German
Improve Your Italian
Improve Your Spanish
Improving Your Employability

Indian Head Massage
Indonesian
Instant French
Instant German
Instant Greek
Instant Italian
Instant Japanese
Instant Portuguese
Instant Russian
Instant Spanish
Internet, The
Irish
Irish Conversation
Irish Grammar
Islam
Italian
Italian Conversation
Italian Grammar
Italian Phrasebook
Italian Starter Kit
Italian Verbs
Italian Vocabulary
Japanese
Japanese Conversation
Java
JavaScript
Jazz
Jewellery Making
Judaism
Jung
Kama Sutra, The
Keeping Aquarium Fish
Keeping Pigs
Keeping Poultry
Keeping a Rabbit
Knitting
Korean
Latin
Latin American Spanish
Latin Dictionary
Latin Grammar
Latvian
Letter Writing Skills
Life at 50: For Men
Life at 50: For Women

Life Coaching
Linguistics
LINUX
Lithuanian
Magic
Mahjong
Malay
Managing Stress
Managing Your Own Career
Mandarin Chinese
Mandarin Chinese Conversation
Marketing
Marx
Massage
Mathematics
Meditation
Middle East Since 1945, The
Modern China
Modern Hebrew
Modern Persian
Mosaics
Music Theory
Mussolini's Italy
Nazi Germany
Negotiating
Nepali
New Testament Greek
NLP
Norwegian
Norwegian Conversation
Old English
One-Day French
One-Day French – the DVD
One-Day German
One-Day Greek
One-Day Italian
One-Day Portuguese
One-Day Spanish
One-Day Spanish – the DVD
Origami
Owning a Cat
Owning a Horse
Panjabi
PC Networking for Small
  Businesses

Personal Safety and Self
  Defence
Philosophy
Philosophy of Mind
Philosophy of Religion
Photography
Photoshop
PHP with MySQL
Physics
Piano
Pilates
Planning Your Wedding
Polish
Polish Conversation
Politics
Portuguese
Portuguese Conversation
Portuguese Grammar
Portuguese Phrasebook
Postmodernism
Pottery
PowerPoint 2003
PR
Project Management
Psychology
Quick Fix French Grammar
Quick Fix German Grammar
Quick Fix Italian Grammar
Quick Fix Spanish Grammar
Quick Fix: Access 2002
Quick Fix: Excel 2000
Quick Fix: Excel 2002
Quick Fix: HTML
Quick Fix: Windows XP
Quick Fix: Word
Quilting
Recruitment
Reflexology
Reiki
Relaxation
Retaining Staff
Romanian
Running Your Own Business
Russian
Russian Conversation

Russian Grammar
Sage Line 50
Sanskrit
Screenwriting
Second World War, The
Serbian
Setting Up a Small Business
Shorthand Pitman 2000
Sikhism
Singing
Slovene
Small Business Accounting
Small Business Health Check
Songwriting
Spanish
Spanish Conversation
Spanish Dictionary
Spanish Grammar
Spanish Phrasebook
Spanish Starter Kit
Spanish Verbs
Spanish Vocabulary
Speaking On Special Occasions
Speed Reading
Stalin's Russia
Stand Up Comedy
Statistics
Stop Smoking
Sudoku
Swahili
Swahili Dictionary
Swedish
Swedish Conversation
Tagalog
Tai Chi
Tantric Sex
Tap Dancing
Teaching English as a Foreign
    Language
Teams & Team Working
Thai
Theatre
Time Management
Tracing Your Family History
Training

Travel Writing
Trigonometry
Turkish
Turkish Conversation
Twentieth Century USA
Typing
Ukrainian
Understanding Tax for Small
    Businesses
Understanding Terrorism
Urdu
Vietnamese
Visual Basic
Volcanoes
Watercolour Painting
Weight Control through Diet &
    Exercise
Welsh
Welsh Dictionary
Welsh Grammar
Wills & Probate
Windows XP
Wine Tasting
Winning at Job Interviews
Word 2003
World Cultures: China
World Cultures: England
World Cultures: Germany
World Cultures: Italy
World Cultures: Japan
World Cultures: Portugal
World Cultures: Russia
World Cultures: Spain
World Cultures: Wales
World Faiths
Writing Crime Fiction
Writing for Children
Writing for Magazines
Writing a Novel
Writing Poetry
Xhosa
Yiddish
Yoga
Zen
Zulu

writing for children

allan frewin jones & lesley pollinger

- Do you want to know more about the writing process?
- Are you eager to develop your talent and improve your skills?
- Do you want to find out about the industry and get published?

Writing for Children is the ideal practical handbook for any aspiring writer of children's books. Drawing on their own experiences, the authors offer you a professional's insight into the process of writing for children. Key points are demonstrated with a comprehensive range of examples and each chapter ends with suggested exercises to encourage you to apply what you have read and develop your own skills.

Allan Frewin Jones is a full-time writer of children's books and **Lesley Pollinger** is an author's agent and lecturer.